Countdown to Poetry Writing

This guide provides all the support you need in helping pupils to improve their poetry writing. *Countdown to Poetry Writing* is a comprehensive and flexible resource that you can use in different ways. It includes:

▶ Stand-alone modules that cover all the essential aspects of writing a poem, including word play, use of metaphor, rhyme and many others;

▶ A countdown flowchart providing an overview showing how modules are linked and how teachers can progress through them with the pupils;

▶ Photocopiable activity sheets for each module that show how to make the decisions and solve the problems that all writers face along the road from first idea to finished piece of work;

▶ Teacher's notes for modules, with tips and guidance, including how modules can be used in the classroom, links to other modules and curriculum links, and advice on helping and guiding pupils in their writing;

▶ A self-study component so that children can make their own progress through the materials, giving young writers a sense of independence in thinking about their work and offering built-in scaffolding of tasks so that less experienced or less confident children get more support from the resource;

▶ 'Headers' for each module showing where along the 'countdown path' you are at that point.

In short *Countdown to Poetry Writing* saves valuable planning time and gives you all the flexibility you need – teachers might want to utilise either the self-study or 'countdown' aspects of the book, or simply dip into it for individual lesson activities to fit in with their own programmes of work.

A former teacher, **Steve Bowkett** is now a full-time writer, storyteller, educational consultant and hypnotherapist. He is the author of more than forty books, including *Jumpstart! Creativity* and *Imagine That*.

Developing pupils' writing abilities boosts their confidence, creates enjoyment and relevance in the task and cultivates a range of decision-making and problem-solving skills that can then be applied across the curriculum. The Countdown series provides all the support you need in helping pupils to improve their prose, poetry and non-fiction writing.

Countdown to Creative Writing

Steve Bowkett

978–0–415–46855–8

Forthcoming title in the series

Countdown to Non-fiction Writing

Steve Bowkett

978–0–415–49259–1

Countdown to Poetry Writing

Step by step approach to writing techniques for 7–12 years

Steve Bowkett

Routledge
Taylor & Francis Group

LONDON AND NEW YORK

First published 2009
by Routledge
2 Park Square, Milton Park, Abingdon, Oxon OX14 4RN

Simultaneously published in the USA and Canada
by Routledge
711 Third Avenue, New York, NY 10017, USA

Routledge is an imprint of the Taylor & Francis Group, an informa business

© 2009 Steve Bowkett

Typeset in Frutiger and Sassoon Primary by
Florence Production Ltd, Stoodleigh, Devon

British Library Cataloguing in Publication Data
A catalogue record for this book is available from the British Library

Library of Congress Cataloging in Publication Data
Bowkett, Stephen.
   Countdown to poetry writing: step-by-step approach to writing
   techniques for 7–12 years/Steve Bowkett.
       p. cm.
   1. Poetry – Study and teaching (Elementary)   2. Poetry –
   Study and teaching (Secondary)   3. Creative writing – Study
   and teaching.   I. Title.
   PN1101.B69 2009
   808.1'071 – dc22   2008038510

ISBN10: 0–415–47752–2 (pbk)

ISBN13: 978–0–415–47752–9 (pbk)

Contents

Acknowledgements

I would like to thank James Trinder (age 6) and Daniel Netherwood (age 8) of the Lady Lane Park Preparatory School for permission to use their excellent poems and the Airedale Writers' Circle for introducing us. Also my grateful thanks to Tim Harding and to performance poet Mark Gwynne Jones for his valuable advice.

Introduction

There are many advantages in encouraging pupils to create poetry, not least that in trying to write it pupils become more competent at interpreting and analysing it. The idea of 'poetry' can also be used very broadly, which means that there is always something in it to engage a pupil at any level. Further benefits are listed below. Hopefully you will find that this book supports them in a practical and enjoyable way:

▶ Writing poetry creates more flexible and creative thinking and broadens perception.

▶ It also develops symbolic (representational) thinking. The understanding that linguistic descriptions are always *interpretations* of things has many powerful repercussions.

▶ Poetry offers a satisfying vehicle for the expression of feelings. A poem not only acts as a 'release valve' for an emotional charge, but also creates a permanent record of the experience. People, places and occasions that might otherwise have been forgotten stay with us in powerful and personal ways through the poetry we write.

▶ Poetry develops the senses and 'refines the sensibilities'. Before searching for the words to express a feeling, we need to *pay attention* to the things around us and to ourselves. Once we listen, we hear. Once we look, we see.

▶ Poetry (reading it as well as writing it) gives us access to things that are otherwise immeasurable or inexpressible. Our deepest thoughts, questions and intuitions can more clearly be expressed poetically than perhaps in any other way.

▶ Poetry builds our understanding of, and ability to use, the natural patterns and cadences of human speech. This develops the power of the voice as a tool for communication.

▶ Every word counts in a poem, so the endeavour to write poetry improves our writing generally.

▶ The act of synthesis sharpens our analytical abilities. When pupils try to frame their thoughts poetically, they often become more appreciative of other people's efforts.

▶ Poetry helps pupils to become unafraid of ideas and words, a vital prerequisite for effective education.

How to use the flowchart

The 'countdown' idea gives structure to the book. You will see from the flowchart on the facing page that ideas, techniques and activities are offered in a certain sequence that I think most usefully guides young writers towards being able to craft meaningful poetry that they can take pride in. However, the book is also modular, so that you (and the pupils) might decide to dip in and try an activity as a stand-alone game or as part of a different programme of work that you have discovered or devised. You'll also see that the way the activities are written up speak to the pupils directly: you can reproduce these pages as activity sheets and/or scan them into the school's intranet, so that different pupils can access the resources according to their own personal progress through the material. Teacher's notes accompany many of the modules and aim to suggest ways of extending the activities.

Extra material for teachers and students can be found on the Routledge website, www.routledge.com/professional/9780415477529. This is indicated by an asterisk * against the relevant modules. There is also a library of sample poems referred to in a number of the modules, which act as examples of the techniques that are discussed in the book. These may be viewed online or printed for classroom use. I have referred to work by a number of other poets and at times suggested searching for these on the Internet. All of the poems can easily be found. However, please be aware of copyright and fair usage issues. A helpful website full of good advice is www.umuc.edu/library/copy.shtml.

Useful classroom tips

Finally, in helping the pupils to work towards finding their own poetical voice I urge you to bear these points in mind:

▶ The words of a pupil's poem, however few or faltering or inadequate, are likely to be the outcome of a great deal of thought. Acknowledge that effort. Value it before you evaluate.

▶ Share the experience. Sit and write poetry yourself. This not only provides great insight into what you're asking the pupils to do, but will help to give them more confidence as they try it for themselves.

▶ Enthusiasm communicates. When you are unafraid of ideas and engage with words playfully, you are modelling the very attitude that will form a solid platform for the pupils' own efforts.

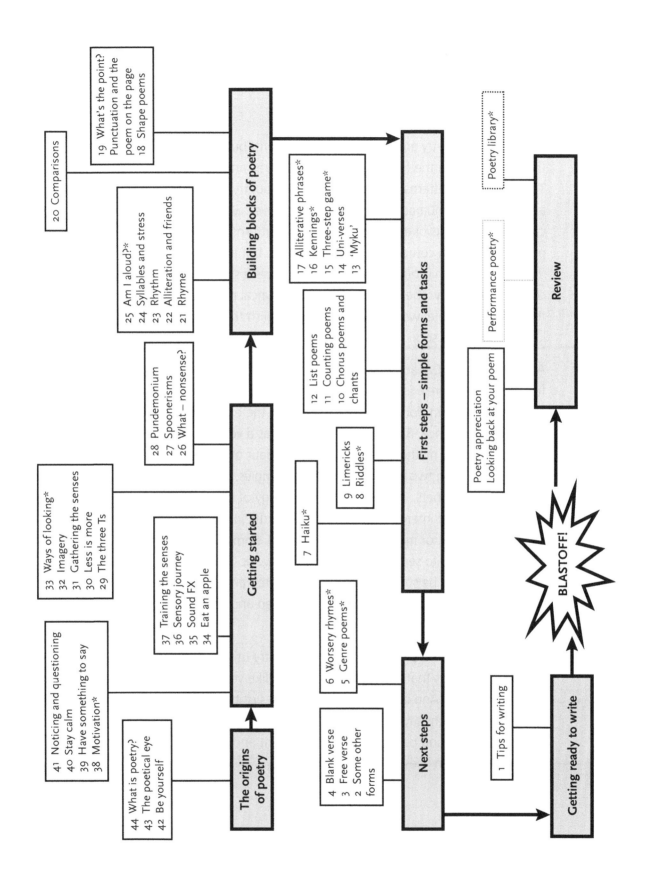

20 Comparisons

19 What's the point? Punctuation and the poem on the page
18 Shape poems

Building blocks of poetry

25 Am I aloud?*
24 Syllables and stress
23 Rhythm
22 Alliteration and friends
21 Rhyme

28 Pundemonium
27 Spoonerisms
26 What – nonsense?

33 Ways of looking*
32 Imagery
31 Gathering the senses
30 Less is more
29 The three Ts

Getting started

37 Training the senses
36 Sensory journey
35 Sound FX
34 Eat an apple

41 Noticing and questioning
40 Stay calm
39 Have something to say
38 Motivation*

44 What is poetry?
43 The poetical eye
42 Be yourself

The origins of poetry

17 Alliterative phrases*
16 Kennings*
15 Three-step game*
14 Uni-verses
13 'Myku'

First steps – simple forms and tasks

12 List poems
11 Counting poems
10 Chorus poems and chants

Poetry library*

Performance poetry*

Review

Poetry appreciation
Looking back at your poem

9 Limericks
8 Riddles*

7 Haiku*

6 Worsery rhymes*
5 Genre poems*

Next steps

4 Blank verse
3 Free verse
2 Some other forms

BLASTOFF!

1 Tips for writing

Getting ready to write

The origins of poetry

The origins of poetry are mysterious and ancient, but what seems to be clear is that its roots lie in the fusion of words and music and, quite probably, dance. The organising patterns that we recognise as poetry exploit the natural rhythms and measures of human speech, which fit so well with the power of music to create mood and evoke emotion. Repeated patterns of sound, memorable and powerful, are also compelling: we cannot help but join in. This gives song a 'binding effect' on groups of people and creates a strong sense of belonging and communal identity. The regularity of musical-lyrical patterns aids memory and they are predictable; we can anticipate with relish the melodies and lines that we know are coming soon.

According to the Canadian poet and thinker Grant Schuyler, the words–music fusion of poetry grew in sophistication and reached a peak with the epic and 'mini-epic' (epyllion) forms of Ancient Greece, the earliest for which we have any written evidence. Bardic poetry was used as a vehicle to record and communicate the mythology and heroic grandeur of the nation; Homer's *Iliad* and *Odyssey* being the two most outstanding examples. Soon afterwards bards came to be known as poets, 'makers' – the etymology of poem is *poieo*, 'a thing made or created' (linked interestingly with the Sanskrit *cinoti*, 'he heaps up' – perhaps event upon event, or meaning upon meaning). Some time after Homer, music and words began to separate. Poems were now no longer exclusively lyrics (words created to be sung to the music of a lyre), and poets became the makers of spoken vocal patterns, which have diversified and flourished up to the modern day.

A great deal of more sophisticated 'adult' poetry utilises and develops the measured patterns that are so obvious in childlike verse: the very idea of metre is 'to measure out'. And even if modern branches of the poetical tradition (the poet-tree you might say) abandon overt rhymes and rhythms, subtle resonances and echoes of sound patterning are still evident and serve as a quiet power behind the written lines.

Modules
44–42

> FOR THE TEACHER

Useful classroom tips

So, coming out of this, what do we immediately need to bear in mind as we encourage pupils to write poetry of their own? In my opinion:

▶ Help them to realise that the basic elements of poetry arise out of what the brain does naturally.

▶ Recall nursery rhymes and be uninhibited when it comes to reciting them (and even singing and dancing to them). Go on, you know you want to.

▶ Emphasise the aural qualities of poetry. This boils down to realising that poetry is still essentially a spoken form of communication much more than it is a visual (written) one. Always encourage pupils to read their work out loud, if only to themselves as they create, compose and later refine their poems.

▶ Point out that ownership of language is every pupil's basic right. We are born with the potential to use words, and any missed opportunity to develop that potential is a terrible waste. We have the same 'right to language' as Shakespeare did, forsooth!

▶ Read and discuss poetry regularly with the pupils. You'll recall my earlier point that the endeavour to create one's own poems sharpens the powers of insight when it comes to commenting on other people's work. I'll have more to say about poetry appreciation and analysis later (see the Review section), but at this stage the primary purpose of looking at lots of poems is to familiarise pupils with a variety of themes, forms and styles.

▶ Be comfortable in the face of not knowing. The meanings of some poems aren't immediately clear. Why should we as adults (and more particularly as teachers) be expected to have all the answers at our fingertips? It has been wisely said that a good teacher is never afraid to say to a pupil 'I don't know – but how might we find out?' Such an attitude encourages further speculation and values a range of interpretations over and above the single 'right' answer (which often comes out of the textbook).

The next three modules introduce what I regard as being some important 'ground rules' when it comes to pupils writing their own poetry. Although the 'countdown' format of the book encourages pupils to make their own decisions and plan their progress through the modules, obviously you will use your judgement in helping individuals to choose wisely (i.e. which modules and in what order).

What is poetry?

> I once met a man from Dundee
> Who said 'Please write a poem for me.'
> I replied 'Don't know how!'
> He said 'We'll find out now –
> So, where to begin? Hmm, let's see . . .'

What is a poem?

What is a poem? Have a think and maybe mention your ideas to your friends. Another important question is, 'What *use* is there in writing poems?' Here are my opinions. Writing a poem:

▶ Allows us an interesting way of looking at something (ourselves, other people, at the big wide world).

▶ Helps us to say how we feel. Not only that, but we have an important and permanent *record* of our feelings. Poems can be significant markers and milestones in our lives.

▶ Gives us a chance to experiment with words. Although maybe 'experiment' is a bit serious. Poems give us a chance to *play* with words.

But what makes poetry interesting?

This is what I believe:

▶ Poetry has a beautiful quality of *sound* that you don't find in other kinds of writing. Did you know that right from very ancient times poems were meant to be spoken and listened to? Originally, experts think, all poems were songs. There were words and music and quite likely dancing all going on at once. Even these days, to read aloud or listen to a poem is a more powerful experience than looking at one on the page.

▶ Poets enjoy using *unusual combinations of words*. Poems can often shock or jolt us into *new ways of looking* because of the originality of their language.

▶ Poetry often creates a great *emotional impact*. Of course other kinds of writing do too, but I think the emotional power of a poem is all the greater when it's spoken and because of the startling way many poems view the world.

▶ Poetry *gets the job done efficiently*. That is to say, in most cases poems explore their subject matter and make their point quickly and directly, using relatively few words – but they are carefully chosen words. And that's important.

So really I'm asking you if you're up for that kind of challenge? I'm asking you if you want to learn some ways of playing with words so that you can put down your thoughts and feelings with great force and beauty? Oh yes, and we'll have some fun as well. Speak with your teacher about where to go next.

The poetical eye

Finding your poetical eye

What I'm calling a poetical eye isn't a real eye of course, but a certain way of looking at things; a way that's unusual and individual and hopefully original. For instance, one of my favourite poets saw a falcon and he called it a 'windhover'. I think that's a brilliant way of seeing it. It makes a picture in my imagination of the bird kind of tilting delicately this way and that on the breeze, before it tips and plunges at the mouse it's hunting.

Here's another example. A friend of mine has a little daughter who wouldn't eat salad until she was told that it was 'crunchy water' and 'munchy juice'. Then she ate the salad! This shows how looking at something in a different way can change the way we feel about it.

Interesting ways of looking at things can be found in ordinary everyday language too. I like the American term 'sidewalk' more than the British word 'pavement' because I think it's more descriptive and makes a clearer picture in my mind. Also I prefer 'billfold' to 'wallet' for the same reason. The idea of bills (paper money) being folded has movement in it, and I can sort of feel it in my hands.

So these are a few of my thoughts about what it means to see with a poetical eye. Obviously our imagination plays a big part too, but once you get into the swing of it and start looking, the world suddenly becomes a much more interesting place.

Activity: Using your poetical eye

Here's an activity to try. In Table 1 you'll find a list of everyday things. They have been glimpsed through the poetical eye and given fresh descriptive names (more or less original ones). Enjoy them, and try out a few variations for yourself . . .

I'd like you to look at a couple of these again – hedgehog, butterfly. Once upon a time these were fresh and original ways of looking at things. Think about them. A hedge-hog. A hog is another name for a pig. A hedge-pig. Why a 'pig' I wonder (though if you've ever *heard* a hedgehog you'll know the answer).

And a butter-fly. Why a 'butter' fly? I suppose it sounds better than a margarine-fly. Can you think of any possible explanations for the name? Actually no one knows for sure. Some people think it comes from the yellow colour of the male brimstone butterfly (brimstone being an old word for sulphur, which is yellow). Other people think butterflies are named after the colour of their poo (oh yuck!), while another theory is the folk belief that butterflies steal milk and butter – 'Quick, grab that butterfly he's getting away with my groceries!'.

And you know, that reminds me of a piece of music by the German composer Johann Strauss II, which he called *Die Fledermaus*. That means 'the bat' or, more truly, 'the fluttermouse'. Don't you think that's a brilliant way of looking at a bat? Mind you, Fluttermouse Man doesn't sound half as tough and brave as Batman!

So another way of strengthening the vision of your poetical eye is to look at ordinary words again, more carefully, and do a bit of research. You'll find out the most incredible things.

OK, coming up is a test to find out how nosy you are. But before then I want you to look at the next module – **Be yourself** (**Module 42**) – because this is very important.

Table 1

Name of object	Another way of looking at it	And your way?
Hedgehog	A waddling pin-cushion	
Clouds	Sky fluff	
Orange juice	Sunlight in a bottle	
Teenage brother	Mouth on legs	
Music	Liquid sound	
Butterfly	A scrap of coloured paper blown by the wind	
Snowflakes	Lacy confetti	
Candyfloss	Nothing-on-a-stick	
Crows	Windblown ashes	
Sun setting	The closing eye of day	

Module 42

Be yourself

You are unique!

Your best poetry will happen when you can be yourself. I think that means:

▶ Being more independent. Making up your mind for reasons you've thought about carefully. Of course it's important to listen to advice, and there's always more to learn, but in the end when we decide things for ourselves we are more truly *individuals*.

▶ Realising that there has never been anyone quite like you before and never will be again. I think that is an amazing idea! It means that the way you look at things and think about things is new and different. And any poem you write shows people those differences.

What comes out of that last point is the notion that, because we are all individuals, what we think and say and write *must be shown respect*. What do you think that word 'respect' means? A dictionary will tell you that in the beginning it meant 'to look back', or 'to look again'. When we look again at something we tend not to take it for granted. We appreciate it and therefore maybe understand it a little bit more. And so we would expect people to respect our thoughts, as we respect theirs.

Activity: Using your imagination

Just before we move on, here's a game. It's best if you play it in a group. Have a look at Figure 1. This is the question – What could that be? What does it remind you of? See how many ideas you all come up with in a minute or two. When you're done ask yourself: Out of all of those ideas, which is the right one? And which is the best one?

If you thought 'any of them' you've got the point of what I've been trying to say. Now skedaddle over to your next module choice.

Figure 1

Noticing and questioning

Helping your pupils be creative

Noticing and questioning are two vital skills in developing creativity of any kind. Use the picture on page 12 (Figure 2) to develop the following abilities in the pupils:

▶ Noticing small details demonstrates focused attention and develops observational skill. Such details artfully used in writing constitute *vivid particularities*. These are images that create a striking image in the mind's eye and often have high emotional impact.

▶ The picture-noticing activity shifts attention inward. Pupils begin to be more aware of the structure and details of their own imaginations. This ability is one aspect of the more general phenomenon of *metacognition*. Literally this means 'thinking about thinking', although a necessary precursor to this is to be able to notice one's mental processes in the first place.

▶ The activity stimulates multisensory thinking – visual, auditory, kinaesthetic. Any activity that encourages multisensory thinking opens up more potential learning strategies for any pupil and improves the flexibility of their imagination.

▶ Encouraging the pupils to ask open questions demonstrates the value of exploring many different possibilities. This kind of questioning also invites interpretations, which can then be discussed, justified, argued for and against – and always respected.

▶ The use of a picture stimulus can introduce the notion that things do not have to be 'literally so'; in other words they can be figuratively true. Guiding pupils towards figurative interpretations of the picture and asking open questions along the way set the stage for the exploration of metaphor and other figurative expressions later. A few such questions that you might find useful are:

  – Does the picture show a real place? What do we mean by 'real'? If it's not real, why do you think the artist wanted to draw it?
  – If this picture told us something about the future of the human race, what might it be?
  – If this picture said something important about your life, what do you learn?
  – If the hare (or maybe it's a rabbit) turned around and looked back down the path, what do you think he would see? (One boy I met in a school said 'Us!' which was a perfectly reasonable response.)
  – What do you think the hare will do next and why?

Another useful ploy is to put the pupils into groups and ask each group to think of a few questions about the picture. Then spend some time exploring answers.

Useful classroom tip

If you wanted to repeat this kind of activity a useful resource is *The Mysteries of Harris Burdick*. These are a series of intriguing black and white drawings that evoke the same kind of wonder as, and invite similar questions to, Stella Hender's startling picture of 'Hare and Cosmos'.

Courtesy of the artist, Stella Hender

Figure 2

Noticing and questioning

How nosy are you? I don't mean sticking your nose into other people's business but, rather, how much do you notice and how often do you ask questions. By the way, I wonder why it's called 'nosiness' when really what I'm thinking about is using your eyes and ears? I suppose calling it 'eye-siness' or 'ear-iness' sounds a bit odd. Never mind.

Activity: Check your NQ

Let's check your NQ (nosiness quotient). Ask your teacher to show you Figure 2. Take a look at the picture:

▶ Notice six things that interest or puzzle you. What are they?

▶ Pretend the picture is in colour. When you've seen at least one colour in your imagination tell your teacher and classmates.

▶ Begin to hear sounds coming out of the picture. Turn up the volume. When you hear sounds, explain what you're listening to.

▶ Now take a slow, deep breath and, in your imagination, *step into the picture*. Stand right there beside the hare. What do you smell? Touch things. What do they feel like? Turn slowly around and notice new things. What are they?

▶ Check the colours and sounds again as you stand inside the picture. Do you notice any changes? Any more sounds and colours?

▶ If you could ask the hare two really important questions what would they be? What do you think the hare would say back to you?

▶ If this was a story, what do you think led up to this point? What might happen next?

▶ If you could describe this picture in no more than ten words, what would you say?

By the way, I wrote my own poem about this picture. If you want to read it go to www.routledge.com/professional/9780415477529.

Take it further

OK, I'm convinced. You're very nosy. Where to next?

▶ If you want to learn to feel very still and settled blink sideways through space to **Stay calm (Module 40)**.

▶ If you'd like to think about some ideas for poems, leap over to modules **Have something to say (Module 39)** and then **Motivation (Module 38)**.

▶ If you want to do some more work on seeing colours and hearing sounds in your imagination, go to the next block of modules and start with **Training the senses (Module 37)**.

Stay calm

Being relaxed

Being able to calm the mind can aid creativity by developing the ability to focus the attention outwardly or inwardly. 'Inward noticing' is a key aspect of metacognition – thinking about one's own thinking.

Such a condition of stillness and absorption-in-reverie has been called the state of *relaxed alertness*. Here the logical-linear conscious mind gives up *trying*, lets go of effort and simply notices the flow of information that seems to come 'out of the blue'. This is the state that generates the so-called 'Aha!' experience or 'Eureka moment', when some new possibility, direction or understanding suddenly pops into awareness. Here one notices material that has already been subconsciously assimilated; often fresh ideas that are the outcome of new associations which usually cannot be logically forced or forged in any methodical way.

Creating a calm classroom

There are many ways of doing this, but one of the most immediate and effective is to use breathing. Breathing usually happens quite automatically, and yet it's easy to 'take conscious control' and deliberately slow, deepen and hold the breath and to pace the inflow and exhalation. Because breathing is connected to the whole physiology, slowing the breath usually has a direct, positive effect on reducing tension, and lowering the heart rate and even blood pressure, especially if combined with the mental techniques outlined in the pupils' module.

Useful classroom tips

It's important that you should direct the calming sessions until all of the pupils are familiar with how it works. Note these guidelines before you begin:

▶ Explain to the pupils that you will be asking them to notice and then change the way they breathe and that this will be a very comfortable and calming thing to do.

▶ Make sure that the environment is right. The temperature should be comfortable, and the room should be airy. The fewer distractions that are around, the better (sometimes difficult to achieve in a school, I know). Some teachers prefer to have soothing music playing in the background, but this isn't essential.

Module 40

▶ Insist that this is to be a 'quiet time' of about ten minutes. Each pupil should be noticing their own breathing and the thoughts going on in their head. No one should be silly or distract anyone else.

▶ Explain that the pupils must follow your instructions carefully. If any pupil doesn't want to take part, then they must sit out and not disturb the rest.

▶ At the end of a session give the pupils a few minutes to chat about their experience. Suggest to them that in future, even when they *think* about their calming breathing, they can feel relaxed straightaway.

Note: If a pupil feels light-headed during the session it's probably because they are 'over-breathing' or hyperventilating. Get the pupil to breathe into a paper bag placed over their nose and mouth. If any pupil already has respiratory problems, consult the parent about the advisability of the pupil doing the session.

Stay calm

Have you noticed your breathing at all today? Maybe not, because it's something that happens 'all by itself'. But you know that once you've noticed your breathing you can change it on purpose. It's easy to make your breathing slower (or faster, although that can make you feel faint), or even to hold your breath if you want to (although that can make you turn red, then blue). This module is all about having that sort of control.

Have you also noticed that when you're nervous or anxious your breathing probably gets faster and shallower (higher up in your chest)? And that when you feel calm your breathing is slower and lighter? That's the kind of breathing we're going to practise now.

Activity: Calming breathing

Your teacher will tell you what to do, but I'm writing these instructions down for you to read first. After you've done so, tell your teacher if you're not happy about doing this 'calming breathing':

▶ First off, sit comfortably. You don't need to be completely still. If you have an itch, scratch it. If you want to sneeze, have a tissue ready! But don't fidget if you can help it.

▶ Notice yourself. Are you frowning? If yes, let the frown fade away. Are your shoulders hunched or tensed? If yes, let them relax. Are your hands clenched? If yes, open them out and turn them palms-up in your lap. If your stomach muscles are clenched let them relax even if that makes your belly sag a little (as mine does all the time).

▶ Now notice your breathing. Don't change it, just notice it happening all by itself. Notice if you are breathing higher up in your chest or deeper down nearer your stomach. Notice if your breathing is shallow or deep, faster or slower. If you are breathing through your mouth right now, are you able to change it to breathe through your nose?

▶ Now do one big slow breath in (inhaling) until you think your lungs are full. Now do one big slow breath out (exhaling) until you feel your lungs are empty.

▶ Do another one of those big slow breaths in – then hold it, one . . . two . . . three – and a big slow breath out. Can you do two more? Great if you can. Then go back to breathing normally.

▶ As you breathe normally, if you're breathing through your nose, notice the cool air in your nostrils. Can you concentrate on how the air feels *just as it enters your nostrils*? You need to be very attentive and quiet to do this. If you have to breathe through your mouth (if your nose is blocked, for instance), notice the cool air on your tongue. Follow the air as it flows down over the back of your mouth and down your windpipe to your lungs. Keep noticing like this for about a minute.

▶ Now, as you breathe normally, imagine that the air going into your lungs is a *white light*. Use your imagination and see that light in your mind, streaming through your nose or mouth and going deep down into your lungs.

Imagining colours and sounds

Here's a tip: if you have trouble seeing colours in your imagination, pretend that the white light is a sound, like a musical note. Then you can *hear* the air flowing into your lungs. If you can neither see nor hear the air in your imagination, just concentrate on how it feels as it streams into your lungs:

▶ Concentrate in this way for about a minute. Then pretend that the air coming out of your lungs is a *blue light*. It's blue because it's full of all the stresses and strains, worries and aches and pains that might have been stuck there inside you. If you can't see the light, hear it – it's a different sound from your inhaling breath. Or feel it as being different. But in any case it's carrying away any and all of your tensions and bad thoughts, so that as you breathe out you can feel yourself relaxing more and more. Concentrate in this way for about a minute.

▶ Now keep using your imagination, but do the white-light-in and the blue-light-out. Notice that you feel calmer and more settled and relaxed with each full breath you take. Do this for about a minute.

▶ Now notice the other pupils and your teacher and the classroom. Well done.

And you know if you do this kind of breathing each day, just for a few minutes, you'll feel much more relaxed than you did before you started. And eventually, just by *thinking* about this kind of deep slow breathing, you'll feel more settled.

The reason why we wanted you to learn this breathing technique is because it helps you to notice the ideas that can easily pop up in your mind. Usually, if you struggle to have ideas or get tense about it, they won't come. But if you just let go and relax, the ideas appear all by themselves. Don't you think that's pretty good – having ideas and feeling so relaxed at the same time?

Of course we don't just 'have ideas'. They have to be *about* something. And certainly as far as poetry is concerned, the best ideas are about things that are important to you or that you feel strongly about. Usually these two go together.

That's what we're going to explore now, so hey, drift calmly over to the next module . . .

Have something to say/ motivation

Encouraging feelings

I can remember an English teacher of mine telling us about her husband, who was a poet. 'But he hasn't written anything for months,' she explained, ' because he's too happy at the moment.' That didn't make much sense to me until I hit the hormonal stormtide of my teens and I was suddenly full of confusion and longing, anger and outrage and the general angst of adolescence. Then the urge to express my emotions was very strong indeed, and it seemed natural to keep (intensely private) diaries and, since I was studying English anyway, to write poetry.

Those early efforts are painful to read now, not because they bring back memories particularly but because they are *so bad*, which is to say, amateurish and fumbling and overblown. But what they lacked in elegance and style they made up for in strength of feeling and in sincerity. They were my own deeply heartfelt thoughts about the things in my life back then that affected me. They were clumsy but they were sincere.

Now I think that this is important, because it's all very well teaching pupils about the techniques of writing poetry, but simply putting a theme in front of them and telling them to make a poem about it is likely to produce some pretty lightweight and empty results; empty, that is, of the passion that drives the individual to action. This isn't to say that the pupils must be intense and driven and in the throes of some overwhelming emotion to write reasonable poetry. These days I write plenty of light stuff just for fun. But if part of our purpose is to raise pupils' awareness of the power of poetry, then they need to appreciate that *authentic* writing grows out of emotional ground and that trying to express our feelings through poetry is a wonderfully effective way of dealing with them.

Module
39

Have something to say

Be interested

I can remember when I was a kid at school the teacher put up a picture of some mountains and told us to write a poem about them. I found that really difficult because I wasn't interested. And because of that I couldn't think of anything to say, well at least not much. What I actually wrote was:

Here are some mountains, mighty and tall.
They just stand about and go nowhere at all.
Look at these mountains, rocky and grey.
They look very high. I might climb them one day.

I got 5/10, and the teacher's comment was 'Quite good'. I thought she was being very kind.

What I'm trying to explain is that your best poetry will come when you write about something that at least interests you or, even better, something that's important to you. That's how it works for me anyway.

Finding a topic

What is important to you? Will you give that some thought and make a few notes? You don't need to show anyone, because sometimes what's most important to us is also very private. Lots of things are important to me but I'll only mention a couple:

▶ When I was about thirteen a girl in our class got leukaemia, which is a cancer of the blood. Her name was Donna. Despite her treatment and the fact that she fought so very hard, after about six months Donna died of her illness. About a year later I happened to mention Donna during a conversation I was having, and a couple of my friends said 'Donna who?'. *They had already forgotten about her!* I thought that was outrageous and terribly sad. Some years later I wrote a poem about Donna so that I at least would never forget her. If you want to read it, it's at www.routledge.com/professional/9780415477529 and it's called 'Donna Didn't Come Back'.

▶ Something else that's important to me is people setting a good example. When I was a schoolteacher I was talking to a pupil's parents at a parents' evening. One lady had caught her son swearing and she really yelled at him about it. 'And I **** well told him that if I **** heard him swearing again I'd knock his **** head off!' I tried really hard to stop myself from laughing. Another lady grumbled that her daughter wasn't making much progress at reading. When I asked about this further, it turned out that neither Mum nor her partner had ever read stories to their daughter, or bought her books, or asked her what books she read at school. So what can you expect? Eventually I wrote a poem about this ridiculous idea of 'do as I say not as I do'. I called it 'Don't' and it's at www.routledge.com/professional/9780415477529.

Take it further

▶ You can tell, I hope, that I feel strongly about these things. To explore feelings a bit further hurry over to the next module, **Motivation** (**Module 38**) – if you can be bothered.

Motivation

Getting motivated

The word motivation means 'to be moved'. It's also linked with 'emotions', which are our thoughts and feelings. That makes sense to me because, often, strong feelings stir us to action, while giving thought to what's important generates those powerful emotions.

So as well as asking yourself 'What is important to me?', you can think about what creates strong feelings in you, which can form a good topic for a poem. Later in the book, when we look at the various forms that poems can take, you'll be able to practise creating different kinds of poems, and you might choose feelings as a theme. But if you'd like to explore the idea now, here are a couple of techniques:

▶ Create a simple list of things that make you feel a certain way. For instance, here are some things that irritate me:

- people talking loudly on mobile phones
- charity collectors rattling tins under my nose
- getting caught out in the rain
- most adverts on TV
- restaurant menus written in another language with no English translation
- weak tea
- dog poo in the streets (and cat poo come to that!)
- selfish drivers
- queue jumpers
- junk mail.

Note: Because I'm a grumpy old guy this list was originally four pages long, but my wife made me shorten it. What else irritates me? Oh yes, long lists!

Using your thoughts

Now, you'll notice that I haven't tried to make my list into a poem. I haven't tried to shape it or refine it. I just let the ideas come out. I've found that not trying to create a poem to start with helps me, because I'm not attempting to do everything at once. I have the basic ideas first and then I can begin to shift them around and form them into the poem I want:

▶ Another idea is to take a feeling and have ideas about it using a word grid such as the example in Table 2. The idea is to put your chosen feeling into the title of your poem. I'll use happiness as my example. Then you use a dice to choose words off the grid at random. Roll the dice twice to choose a word. Count the first number from left to right and then the second number upwards.

So 3–4 gives us *chain*, 6–2 gives us *princess of the stars* and so on. Each word gives you an idea for completing one line of your poem. Here's my effort:

Table 2

castle	snow	axe	waterfall	dragon	two-headed dog
forest	mask	clashing rocks	winged horse	backwards walking man	jewel
questions	path	chain	labyrinth	storm	comedy/ tragedy
wolf	three friends	shooting star	leaves	hunter's moon	clouds
mountains	lost cave	tunnel	wheat	wilderness	princess of the stars
magic spell	wise one	dream	fairy	the maker	demon

Happiness is the maker of all things bright (5–1)
Happiness comes when not all questions need answers (1–4)
Happiness is the thread that guides me through the labyrinth (4–4)
Happiness is the castle's drawbridge let down to welcome me in (1–6)
Happiness is the path that leads me back to myself (2–4).

Again I wasn't trying to force the ideas to come, but simply kept my mind focused on how the words in the grid reminded me of happiness. If you'd like to see another example, this time written by Year 5 pupils, go to www.routledge.com/ professional/9780415477529.

So use your feelings to motivate yourself to write. Poetry is a great way of expressing how you feel.

Now let's move on to the next block of modules.

Training the senses

A friend of mine once said to me, as we walked around town, 'Have you noticed there's a lovely lemony light around today?' I hadn't until then, but I've never forgotten that simple and evocative description. It sums up the notion of the 'poetical eye' wonderfully, which is one that:

▶ notices fine distinctions and subtle differences;

▶ sees the unique in the ordinary;

▶ reflects the individual perspective of the observer.

Benefits of the poetical eye

Being able to appreciate the special in the mundane creates an emotional soil out of which the language of poetry can grow. The Victorian Jesuit poet Gerard Manley Hopkins coined the term *inscape*, which is each created thing's unique inner landscape, expressed by the very fact of its *being* or, as Hopkins phrased it, 'selving – going itself'. One of the achievements of poetry is the expression, once recognised, of 'what each thing speaks and spells' – its essential self.

Motivating pupils to write

Once a pupil notices something new or different, he or she immediately has a subject to write about. Also, and importantly, that individual observation gives the pupil ownership of the idea, which leads to increased self-confidence when it comes to talking or writing about it. More generally, refining the senses through active noticing reverses the way that so much in our culture serves to blunt the sensibilities – to desensitise the way we look at and appreciate the world.

Training the senses

Being curious

In a little book I wrote once (called *Philosophy Bear and the Big Sky*) there was a character named Pinkerton who was a very curious cat. She was curious in the sense that she was nosy and loved to notice things. Pinkerton enjoyed chasing leaves and would always try to catch two together. Then she became very quiet and still, because she was noticing the differences between those two leaves. How many differences between two leaves could you notice, I wonder? Maybe you'll test yourself and have a go some time today?

Activities: *Training your senses*

What I've called training the senses is all about noticing. If you worked through the module **Noticing and questioning** (**Module 41**) you'll already have met this idea. Now it's time to take the next step. Try these activities:

▶ Look around the classroom (or wherever you are) and notice something that's blue. Now find as many different shades of blue as you can. Try this using a different colour too.

▶ Advice: Only attempt this if you don't get easily embarrassed! Find a partner and look into their eyes. Notice as many details as possible about the colour and patterning of their eyes. Now write a short description while they do the same for your eyes.

▶ Select an ordinary small object – a pencil, a new book, a pot plant. Smell it carefully. What words come to mind that would help to describe that smell?

▶ Find a peaceful place or ask your teacher to encourage everyone in the class to be quiet for a minute. Listen to the different small sounds that are still going on. No need to do anything else. Just be aware of those little sounds.

▶ Get two pieces of fruit (they can be the same kind of fruit), so two raspberries for example or blueberries, which work particularly well. Eat one of the fruits slowly and carefully, paying close attention to the flavours in your mouth. Take a drink of water. Now eat the second piece of fruit in the same way. What differences do you notice between them?

▶ Your teacher and classmates will need to prepare for this one. Bring something to class that has an interesting (but never unpleasant) smell. A flower, an aromatic oil, a spice, that sort of thing. The idea is that you sniff one of these and notice the thoughts that immediately pop into your mind and jot them down. What works well I've found is if about five or six pupils at a time move around the room from table to table, inviting their classmates to smell the object they've brought. You might find the activity is better if you don't look at the object or know what it is. Just sniff it and notice your thoughts.

This last activity asks you to notice how a smell is linked with your thoughts. Being aware of your thoughts is really important if you want to have good ideas for making poems – so let's practise that a bit more now.

Sensory journey

A sensory journey is a kind of guided narrative that asks pupils to imagine scenes that you suggest to them using all of their senses. Initially the activity is teacher-led. Think of an imaginary journey you want the pupils to make – a walk around town, visiting the zoo, exploring the woods etc. Then break it into a number of steps, with a question attached to each step. See the example in the pupil notes. Encourage the pupils to make a written response to each question, but don't insist on one:

▶ Explain that there are no right answers to the questions.

▶ Responses should be brief and based on first impressions.

▶ No responses need to be made if nothing comes to mind or if the question doesn't interest the pupil.

Allow no more than a minute or so for pupils to jot down their thoughts, which might be just a few disconnected impressions or only a word or two. Certainly there's no need for ideas to be expressed as full sentences.

Once you've taken a class on a few such journeys, pupils can write more for themselves. Extend the activity by linking it with other aspects of 'poetical writing', such as noticing subtle distinctions, or using metaphors, alliteration, onomatopoeia etc.

Sensory journey

Activity: Going on a journey

I want to take you on a journey in your imagination. Below are a number of things I'd like you to think about. As ideas come to mind write them down in a few words. You don't need to worry about complete sentences or even (on this occasion) spelling and punctuation. If no particular thoughts occur to you just move on to the next question.

Note: Your teacher might do this as a whole-class activity and read these questions out to you:

1   Pretend you are old enough to drive. You decide one morning to visit the seaside. You hop into your car and try to start the engine, but it won't start because it's got a bit damp overnight. As the engine tries to fire up you get a strong smell of petrol in the car. Pretend I've never smelt petrol fumes in my life. How would you describe them to me?

2   You sit quietly in the car wondering what to do. It's a showery kind of day, and all of a sudden there's a heavy downpour. You listen to the sound of the rain on the roof of your car. How will you describe that sound (without using words like 'drumming', 'pitter-patter' or 'splish splash')?

3   The rain stops very quickly and the sun comes out. Now your car starts just fine, and you drive to the beach, parking at the top of a gently sloping sand dune. You decide to walk down to the sea but seem to have forgotten your sandshoes so you have to go bare foot. On your way you come to a pebbly section of beach. What does it feel like on the soles of your feet as you walk across that area of pebbles? Try and choose words that make me feel the pebbles on *my* bare feet.

4   You get closer to the sea and can smell the salt water and the seaweed. If I had never smelt the ocean before, how would you describe it to me?

5   You're walking along the shoreline, letting the cool water lap over your feet. You decide to have a drink and, after rummaging in your beach bag, find a bottle of your favourite (non-alcoholic) drink. As you take long refreshing mouthfuls you notice the flavour. What could you say to make *me* taste that drink?

6 Continue on your way until you notice that up ahead some children are flying kites. Look at the way the kites move in the air and the sounds they make. Describe what you see and hear and, if you can, compare the kites to something else. For instance, 'The kites looked like coloured birds swooping around each other, red, blue and green swirling patterns.' Except you can't use that example because it's mine!

7 A little further on you watch the waves rushing up to the shore then falling back, and somehow the ocean reminds you of your whole life. Make a sentence out of that idea. If you have difficulty you might say, 'The ocean was like my whole life because . . . ', and just finish off the line.

8 As you stand there looking out to sea your feet sink into the warm, wet, heavy sand. Feel it on your skin and the sensation of the sand covering your toes. Describe it briefly – without using the words warm, wet or heavy.

9 After walking for some time you decide to return to your car. You dry your feet with a towel and as you stuff it back into your beach bag you come across your sandshoes – you packed them after all. You walk back to the sand dune where your car is parked and, to climb up, use hands and feet to scrabble to the top. Standing there on the dune you notice you have a handful of sand. Let it slip and pour through your fingers and describe that sensation.

10 As the last grains of sand slide from your hand you find yourself holding a delicate little shell, which you decide to take home as a keepsake. Notice its shape and colour. Notice the tiny sounds it makes as you blow gently into the shell's opening. Feel the shape and texture of the shell. Smell it. Now write a sentence or two to give me that same experience.

Take it further

Well done. And now that you've relaxed and enjoyed yourself, let's get on with some work!

▶ If you're interested in sounds particularly, drive over to **Sound FX** (**Module 35**).

▶ If you'd like to eat an apple, paddle across to **Eat an apple** (**Module 34**).

▶ If you want to learn more about different points of view, sand-surf down to **Ways of looking** (**Module 33**).

Module
35

Sound FX

Using sound FX sheets

Before launching this activity with the pupils, look at Figure 3 and note down your first impressions. These might include:

▶ a picture that comes to mind, a scene from memory for instance;

▶ ideas about the words themselves, perhaps some that strike you as loud noises or . . .

▶ quieter sounds, single sounds, multiple sounds etc.;

▶ relatively few impressions; perhaps if you're a very visual thinker you don't immediately conjure up pictures in response to these 'sounds';

▶ if you are a highly developed auditory thinker, the sounds (in your 'mind's ear') as you read the words;

▶ kinaesthetic impressions, such as rough sounds, smooth sounds and sharp sounds.

Or perhaps you're busy gathering impressions that are a mixture of the above. These are the same sorts of experience the pupils will have. Their responses will be useful feedback to you about the kind of thinking they do, such as whether one sensory modality (visual, auditory, kinaesthetic) predominates; whether memories and feelings are easily evoked; what kinds of association they make with the words etc.

Notice also the tendency that some pupils have towards describing sound in other sensory terms. And so we have long and short sounds, high sounds, low, heavy, light, stretched out etc. This phenomenon is explored more fully in **Gathering the senses** (**Module 31**). For now, it's useful just to be aware of it.

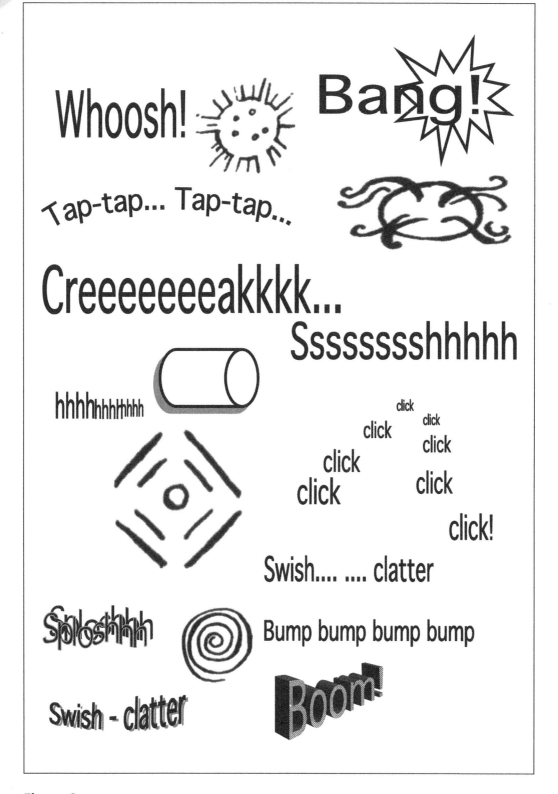

Figure 3

Module
35

Useful classroom tips

'Sound FX' sheets like this are easy to make. The pupils can create their own, for instance, by using the WordArt tool in a Microsoft Word document and by importing a few simple pictures. The most basic use of the activity is to raise the group's awareness of onomatopoeia and other 'auditory' literary devices. But you can also try the following:

▶ Ask the class to pretend that the sounds suggest a particular place and ask them to describe that place. If any pupil needs prompting, say it could be a busy market or a building site or a bonfire party etc.

▶ Ask pupils to put the sounds in order of volume, quiet-to-loud.

▶ Ask pupils to look at the simple images among the sound words. Say 'Pretend that picture is a sound. What do you hear?' If a pupil reports 'hearing' nothing, say 'If that whole picture were a sound what kind of sound could it be?'

▶ Ask the pupils to select a sound and imagine 'holding that sound in your hands. What do you feel?' Suggest size, shape, temperature, texture and so on as necessary.

▶ Ask the group to imagine a place such as a fairground and create a 'sound FX' sheet to suit it.

▶ Help the pupils to refine their auditory sense by asking them to make subtle distinctions. For instance, imagine three puddles. A kid drops a pebble into each of them. They go splish, then splash, then splosh. What's the difference between the puddles?

▶ Begin to encourage pupils to compose sentences that describe and emphasise sounds. This is a good opportunity to introduce or revisit alliteration and assonance. Some examples from pupils I worked with include:

  – The thin eerie creeeeeak of the slowly opening door.

  – Clank-clank-clank of the tin can kicked down the steps.

  – Whoooshhh – BANG! – sparkle – fizz firework embers falling.

  – Click-click-click-click . . . tick-tock Tick-Tock TICK-TOCK the man with the clock hurries away, hurries back – knock knock on the door. What a shock!

▶ Read poems that use sounds elegantly, like the old school favourite, Walter de la Mare's 'The Listeners'. Using such a poem, begin to make the distinction between overtly onomatopoeic words and alliterative phrases that build atmosphere and mood very delicately yet effectively, as in 'fell echoing through the shadowiness of the still house' or the wonderful line 'And how the silence surged softly backward . . .'.

Sound FX

Sounds can be very important in poetry, partly because they add an extra dimension to any description, but also because poetry really is meant to be spoken aloud rather than just looked at on the page. When you read a poem that features lots of sounds, your voice has to make them as you read, thus creating a 'sound landscape' for your listeners to enjoy.

Work with your teacher on the 'sound FX' sheet and then tiptoe silently to the next module.

Eat an apple

Using mind and body

When I talk to pupils about descriptive writing I tell them the story of how I once asked a class to write a short description of an apple. Virtually everyone in the group picked up their pencil and started writing (although some kids stared out of the window instead). One boy however was staring intently at something on his table that was quite invisible to me. After a few moments he picked it up and weighed it gently in his hand, sniffed it, polished it on his jumper and then took a big crunchy bite; chewed, wiped the juice off his chin, bit again then put the apple down and, still munching, began his description. Although he was by no means the most academically able pupil in that class, his description was the most evocative and vivid.

Because the mind and the body are linked, our thoughts influence our physiology. That's easy to demonstrate. Think of a pleasant memory and we smile fondly or laugh: think of an unpleasant occasion and we frown, tense up, our pulse increases and so on. This simple idea forms the basis of the whole positive thinking industry and, on the downside, lies at the heart of many people's highly developed capacity for worry and regret.

Similarly, we can use our bodies to influence our thoughts. Notice how many people use their hands, sometimes very eloquently, as they talk. This is not random gesturing. Their hands are a kind of physical analogue to what's going on in their heads. Have you ever listened to an angler describe their latest catch without measuring out with their hands how big it was (and did you ever believe them)?

Useful classroom tip

The point is that our imaginations are aided by physical movement. We'll explore this further in **Gathering the senses (Module 31)**. For now, as you ask the pupils to 'eat an apple' help them to understand how holding it, sniffing it, biting it and spitting out a stray pip will improve the quality of their description.

Eat an apple

Using your body and your mind

That's what we're going to do now. Not actually but in our imaginations – and some people have such strong imaginations the experience is nearly the same. I remember when I was about seven years old, once a week our teacher would play us classical music and tell us about the composers. I'm sorry to say that I found it incredibly boring. So I would pretend that I had a bag of sweets in my lap and that every sweet was different. I might dip in that bag and pull out a mint or a toffee or a bubblegum ball or a sherbet lemon. And do you know, I could imagine those sweets so clearly that even now, %$^&!-three years later, I can still feel the mint's cool vapours streaming through my nose and down my throat, and my mouth still puckers at the acid sourness of the sherbet lemon:

▶ Our bodies react to our thoughts, and our thoughts react to our bodies. In a moment we'll ask you to write a description of an apple – or another piece of fruit if you prefer . . . Oh, all right then, or of eating a bag of sweets (but swill your mouth with water afterwards). Your teacher will give you some instructions about how to do this – eat the apple I mean, not swill your mouth.

▶ Afterwards I would like you to do a *word web* about the topic of your description. Put the topic word in the middle of a sheet of paper and then have other ideas radiating away from it. These will be thoughts that just pop into your mind about things that remind you of the apple, or whatever it is that you've chosen. I've done part of a word web about my apple to show you what I mean, Figure 4.

▶ Finally, I want you to write five or six lines using some of the ideas from your web. You can put 'Reminds me of . . . ' at the start of each line if that helps you. Here's what I mean.

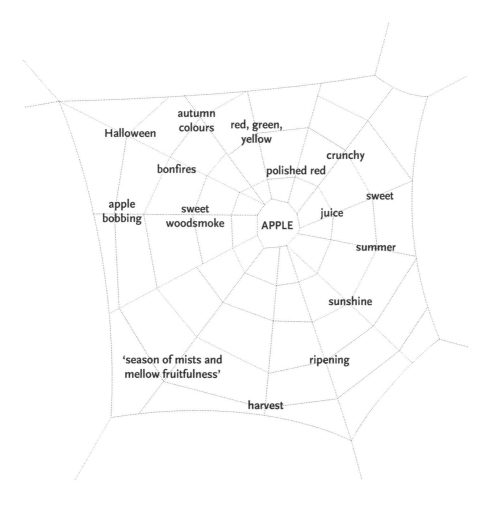

autumn colours
Halloween
red, green, yellow
crunchy
bonfires
polished red
sweet
apple bobbing
sweet woodsmoke
APPLE
juice
summer
sunshine
'season of mists and mellow fruitfulness'
ripening
harvest

Figure 4

Eating an Apple
Reminds me of misty mornings that smell of woodsmoke
Reminds me of busy markets, people and shouting
Reminds me of Halloween, screams and shadows and laughter
Reminds me of sweetness and crunch
Reminds me of summer days wrapped up in that little ball of juice.

Now it's time to move on to the next block of modules. Put your apple core and sweet wrappers in the bin, and let's go.

Ways of looking

Encouraging expression

An effective poem (indeed any creative expression) represents a fresh and insightful perspective. In some cases, the very fact that a pupil is a unique individual means that what they say represents an original point of view. However, sometimes a failure of nerve or a failure of imagination drains the vigour from the pupil's way of looking, and their work becomes pale, derivative and routine. This is not to say that we shouldn't encourage pupils to imitate the techniques and stylistic features of other writers – emulation is an important step on the road to finding one's own voice. But I'm talking about something different, which is a kind of giving up, a laziness in creative endeavour or a fear of 'doing it wrong'. These tendencies must be watched for and countered wherever possible, because they will dampen the pupil's whole thinking process. Conversely, if we can encourage and support individuality of thinking as we ask pupils to play with words and strive towards poetic freshness, such habits of thought will be transferred to all areas of their learning and then beyond school into their lives more generally.

Useful classroom tips

▶ The following module asks pupils to take different points of view as they engage with the picture 'Through the window', Figure 5. Each time they stand in someone else's shoes in this way they are developing empathy – their ability to view the world from another's perspective and appreciate something of how that person feels. This is a useful activity in PSHE/Citizenship programmes of work.

▶ The activity 'Six ways of looking at a . . .' was inspired by Wallace Stevens' poem 'Thirteen Ways of Looking at a Blackbird'. Google it, or see the Bibliography.

Courtesy of the artist, Stella Hender

Figure 5

Module 33

Ways of looking

How strong is your imagination?

One way of measuring the strength of your imagination is by how *original* your way of looking/thinking happens to be. The word original is linked with the word 'origin', which comes from Latin (the language of the Ancient Romans), meaning *to rise*. So if you have an original thought it rises up in your mind for the first time. A truly, completely and absolutely original thought is one that has never been thought of by anyone at all, until now. If you or I ever have a truly original thought we can feel very proud of ourselves.

Activities: Workouts for your imagination

One way of strengthening your imagination then is to deliberately try to see things differently. Here are a few activities to give you some practice:

▶ Look at Figure 5. What do you think is going on between those two people? Make a list of your ideas. Think of as many as you can – it doesn't matter how fantastical, weird or ridiculous they seem. Now pick an idea or one of the options at www.routledge.com/professional/9780415477529 and decide what she could be thinking and what he could be thinking. Write their thoughts in the think bubbles you'll find in Figure 6 (you'll need to get these photocopied and then cut them out).

If you want to do more work on this picture, go to www.routledge.com/professional/9780415477529 for further ideas.

Figure 6

Imagery

What is imagery?

Imagery basically means using language to evoke pictures in the reader's mind. Effective imagery also stirs the emotions and demonstrates the other characteristics of the poetical eye (see **The poetical eye** (**Module 43**)).

Potentially every line of a poem, novel or play conveys an image. A useful activity to try out with the pupils is not just to read out to them but also ask them afterwards what mental pictures they made. Then, on the second reading, have them notice the pictures *as* they listen to the words, i.e. have them be metacognitive about it.

It might be argued that all poetical devices have evolved to create powerful imagery. A strong image is immediately 'impressive' in the important sense of generating memorable pictures-plus-feelings. We remember effective images. And it's significant here to note that to remember means to 're-member', to bring sensations into the members (the limbs and body). A good image is also a *physical event*. It's likely that you can remember immediately a number of impressive images from stories and poems.

In terms of poetry there are too many images for me to make a choice. But one complete poem that still leaves me breathless is Ted Hughes's 'The Express' (from his collection *Moortown*). I am there on the platform gasping as the steam train thunders through, with the blast and slipstream of air that follows. The magic happens every time I read it. I once tried to analyse it to find out how Hughes had done it, then I realised that, as the Japanese say, I was slitting the throat of the skylark to find out how it sang. So I left it alone.

Any poetry reading session that you do with the pupils should look at the imagery of the poems, not so much in the technical sense but vitally on what kind of 'feeling impact' they make; how they 'impress'.

Imagery

You'll know that this word has something to do with 'images' or the pictures that you make in your imagination when you read or listen to stories and poems. The brilliant thing about these is that they allow you to *make your own* images. When we watch TV or go to the cinema, the images are all done for us. I'm not saying books are better than TV, just that it's a different experience.

Thinking about images

When you go about writing your own poems or stories, one of the things you'll have to think about is the imagery you use. I think that the best kind of imagery does the following things:

► It makes a clear picture in the reader's or listener's mind.

► It stirs the emotions.

► It helps the listener to appreciate how *you* see the world.

► It creates some of its effect by the sound of the words as they are spoken.

What do you see?

A clear example of strong imagery is found in a poem by Thomas Hardy (1840–1928). It's called 'The Darkling Thrush'. You can find it easily on the Internet. The first thing to do when you read or listen to poems is to make sure you understand what the individual words mean. So if I were coming to this poem for the first time I'd want to know what coppice, spectre, dregs and desolate mean. A few minutes with a dictionary sorts that out.

Coppice – a little wood of small trees / Spectre – a ghost or phantom / Dregs – what's left at the end or the worthless part, like coffee grounds left at the bottom of the cup / Desolate – barren, lonely, in ruin, uninhabited.

So now I have a picture in my head of a guy leaning on a gate near a small wood. He is by himself and it is wintertime. The word 'desolate' gives me the idea that he is in a lonely place and maybe he is lonely too.

Questioning poetry

But there's more going on here, and so I need to ask further questions and make some guesses.

See how Thomas Hardy compared the frost to a spectre? Why did he pick a ghost when he could have chosen from lots of grey things? Perhaps because a ghost is something dead and to be avoided. And ghosts are sometimes thought of as 'lost souls'. Well that would make them pretty lonely and desolate too. And the way a ghost drifts might be like the mist in the air that you get on frosty days.

So I reckon that Hardy's image is a good one, because it has all of those possible meanings wrapped up in it. I say 'possible meanings' because I don't know if I'm right or not. Part of the pleasure of discussing poetry is to hear about lots of different possible meanings, not to prove who is right or wrong. This is a very important point, and I would like you to bear it in mind.

There are other questions that occur to me too. Here they are, and maybe you'll give them some thought and come up with ideas of your own:

▶ Why, I wonder, does Thomas Hardy use a capital F for Frost?

▶ What does the phrase 'Winter's dregs' mean? How does it help Hardy to create that feeling of loneliness in the listener?

▶ What is 'the weakening eye of day'? In what sense is it getting weaker?

What impresses me is that we can ask so many questions and have so many thoughts about just a few lines of poetry! That's one of the joys of good poetry – there's so much folded up in it. Now here's a trick for making up striking images of your own – drift to the next module.

Gathering the senses

Synaesthesia

The Welsh poet Dylan Thomas once issued an anthology of verse that he had broadcast called *The Colour of Saying*. The title fascinated me even before I came across the phenomenon known as *synaesthesia*. The word literally means 'a gathering of the senses' or 'perceptions brought together' and is the way that some people 'translate' information from one sense into a response through another sense; or make what neuropsychologists call 'a cross-modal association'. Essentially this is a neurological phenomenon, but some researchers make a distinction between that and the sense in which I am using it, as a metaphorical cross-matching of the senses in the imagination. However, the device of cross-matching the senses to create striking imagery is a useful one and is already deeply built into the way we use language.

Colour and mood

Consider for instance the link that we make between colours and moods. Asking even quite young pupils 'What colour is anger?' is not a meaningless question to them. A little further thought will throw up colour links to other feelings such as envy, cowardice and fury, while Sherlock Holmes might well have gone into a 'brown study' and sent London criminals into a 'blue funk'. Beyond that it's easy to find endless examples of what we might call multisensory words. 'Soft' for instance is a touch word (kinaesthetic) and a sound word, while we might talk about the wind as being bitter or sharp or cutting. All of these words have something in common – austere, backbone, big, crisp, earthy, firm, flabby, green, high notes, grip, lean, sharp, silky, soft, steely, undertones. They are all terms used by wine tasters to describe the smell and taste of wine.

Useful classroom tips

Cross-matching the senses in this metaphorical way allows many pupils to use the vocabulary that they already have in a richer and more original way. Develop their ability by trying the following:

▶ Show the class some abstract art and say 'If this were music what would you hear?'.

▶ Play some instrumental music and say 'If this were a place, what is it like?' or 'If this were a person, describe them to me now.'

▶ Encourage comparisons between the sounds of musical instruments in a 'synaesthesic' way. Pupils will already be able to appreciate that adjectives such as high, deep, sharp, low etc. are about space (spatial positioning) as well as about sound, but push the game further. Rattle a tambourine. What colour is the sound? Notice how the colour changes when you ting a triangle. If you could hold the sound of a flute in your hand, how would it feel different from the sound of an oboe? What would you taste if you could chew on the rat-tat-tat of a snare drum?

▶ Turn aromas into sounds and/or colours. Let pupils sniff at spices and aromatic oils and ask them what colour a smell produces or what music it makes.

▶ Systematically forge metaphors by using a theme. Take a link between, say, feelings and time of year. What does a wintry mood feel like? How would you describe an April smile? How might you interpret the description of someone's face that wore an Octobery expression? We'll return to games like these when we come to **Comparisons** (**Module 20**).

Gathering the senses

Mixing your senses

What do these feel like?

- ▶ A feathery breeze
- ▶ A barbed-wire wind
- ▶ A violin wind.

Describe what kind of sounds you hear:

- ▶ A lilac sound
- ▶ A silvery sound
- ▶ A lime green sound.

If you could hold these emotions in your hand, what would they feel like?

- ▶ Frustration
- ▶ Jealousy
- ▶ Delight.

If you had any ideas at all, then something interesting is happening in your mind – you are thinking about one sense (for example sound) by using another sense (for example sight). For me, a silvery sound for instance is light and tinkly and delicate. A lime green sound is loud and raucous. That makes sense to me because if my best friend wore a lime green shirt I'd say that shirt was 'loud'. Loud colours tend to be bright and perhaps outrageous. 'Muted' colours are 'quieter' and blend in. The same word muted is also used to describe sounds.

Cross-matching your senses

Being able to cross-match our senses like this is useful when you want to describe things in interesting and unusual ways. I remember when I was working with a group in a school once and we did this trick where, in our imaginations, we pretended we could step into a picture. There were fireworks in the picture and one girl said 'Oh, I can smell the firework smoke!' I asked her to describe the smell but she couldn't think of anything to say. So I said 'Pretend you could touch the smell. What does it feel like?' She said it was soft and fluffy like cotton wool. Then I asked her to imagine that the smell was a sound and what did she hear? She said 'A soft and whispery note.' Then I asked her to make the smell into a colour and she said it was light purple.

'So describe the smell of the fireworks.' And the girl said, 'It's a soft, fluffy, quiet, whispery light purple smell.' And her teacher gave her a merit point! Later on in a story she wrote she mentioned the *purple cotton-woolly smell of fireworks*. See what she'd done? She looked again at her description and trimmed it down. We'll be looking at that soon, but before then your teacher might want to do a bit more with you on cross-matching the senses.

Less is more

(There are no teacher's notes for this module.)

Choosing your words

In **What is poetry?** (**Module 44**), I said that poetry uses language very effectively. By that I mean it makes the reader's/listener's imagination do lots of work without using many words. Remember how even the first four lines of Thomas Hardy's poem 'The Darkling Thrush' created that vivid picture of the solitary man on a bleak winter's day? That opening also raised lots of questions and could lead to plenty of discussion.

So that's one good thing about writing poetry – usually you don't have to write very much. However, you do have to choose your words carefully so that each one does plenty of work. And you'll find that when you read poems many of them are 'trimmed to the bone', with no words wasted.

Activities: Using words

Let's practise doing that for ourselves. Try these activities:

▶ Pick a topic and write five or six words that seem to 'capture its essence'.
   Tip: there's no need to write in full sentences. Here are a few I did:
   – Lion – fierce, Africa, king, savannah, beast, hunter.
   – Winter – cold, dark, snow, ice, bleak, frost.
   – Tree – tall, gnarled, leaves, roots, fruits.

▶ Next, use your ideas to make a three-word phrase that aims to sum up the topics you've chosen. So:
   – Lion – stately savannah king.
   – Winter – bleak frost months.
   – Tree – enduring fruit giver.

Later on we'll look at two forms of poetry, the *kenning* and the *haiku*. You can glance ahead to them now if you want to. You'll find kennings in **Module 16** and haiku in **Module 7**. Notice how kennings use very punchy two- or three-word phrases to describe things, while haiku poetry, like a few elegant brush strokes on a canvas, suggests a picture.

▶ Now have a go at developing the descriptive phrases you've just thought of. What I'd like you to do is to add a line that says something about what each topic means to you. Or say something further that completes a mental picture. You can alter your original descriptive phrase if necessary. Here's my attempt:

Lion
stately savannah king
rules with quiet power.

Winter
bleak frost months
when life slumbers below.

Tree
fruit giver
endures even to its last
leaf.

As I suggested above, think of these 'mini descriptions' as being like a few brush strokes on a canvas. The words suggest much more than they say.

Take it further

▶ Now you can either move on to **The three Ts** (**Module 29**) which rounds off this block . . .

▶ Or slip into your clown outfit and prepare for some **Pundemonium** (**Module 28**).

Module
29

The three Ts
Theme, tone and technique

(There are no teacher's notes for this module.)

The three Ts give us a useful way of remembering how poems are built.

Theme

The *theme* of a poem is what it's about; the main idea that you're trying to express. It's bigger and deeper than a 'topic'. Sometimes the theme of a poem is obvious and simple. In my poem 'Don't', for example, the theme of the poem is how adults tell kids not to do things when the adults themselves often do far worse things! Perhaps this is an idea you've come across before . . .

Sometimes a poem's theme is not so obvious, or else it's quite a deep idea and the poem suggests different 'layers' that you can explore. With that in mind, what do you think might be the theme or themes of 'Donna Didn't Come Back'? On the surface it's about that poor girl who died and so didn't turn up to school any more. But I also think it touches on the idea that bad things can happen to good people sometimes, apparently for no reason at all. In fact folks have been wrestling with that idea for a long time and, especially if you are religious, it's a hard problem to try to solve.

So another reason why poetry is important is because it explores people's most difficult ideas and most powerful feelings and beliefs.

Tone

The *tone* of a poem is its mood, and also the mood it aims to put you in as you read it. If you checked out Thomas Hardy's 'The Darkling Thrush' and read it right through you'll know that the tone at the start is bleak, dark and despairing. But then, in the middle of that winter landscape a thrush begins to sing because it knows spring is on its way, and that fills Hardy with hope. So the tone at the end is hopeful and full of excited anticipation.

When you've chosen a theme you want to write about, give some thought to the tone it will take. Imagine your tone of voice as you read it. The tone of 'Don't' is angry and cutting but also, at the end, kind of tolerant and pleading. But it didn't have to be like that. I could have made it light-hearted and funny, even though underneath it was dealing with a serious subject. Think about cooking an egg. You can boil it, poach it, fry it, scramble it. Each way of cooking will affect the taste and texture, but really it's still the same egg. So it is when you decide on a particular tone for your poem. It will affect the theme but not turn it into something else.

Technique

Technique means all of the different tricks and devices and forms that poets use to build their poems. You'll know about many of them already: things like rhyme, rhythm, metaphors and different types of verse structure. Looking at those is what much of the rest of this book is about.

But before we get on to that, remember that, while you use the three Ts for creating your own poems, those ideas are also useful for looking at other people's work. In fact when you explore a poem they could be the first three questions you ask:

▶ **Theme** – what is the poem basically about?

▶ **Tone** – what is the 'mood' of the poem? What feelings does the poet want me to have?

▶ **Technique** – how has the poet created those feelings and explored the poem's themes?

Take it further

▶ OK, it's up to you now. You might want to get stuck in straightaway to some basic aspects of technique. If so, make a conga-chain and dance over to the next block of modules – **Building blocks of poetry (Modules 25–18)**.

▶ Or maybe you prefer some light-hearted fun playing with words? If so, laugh yourself silly over to **Pundemonium (Module 28)**.

Pundemonium

This deliberate pun on 'pandemonium' emphasises the idea that, out of the apparent chaos and confusion of play, come the order and discernment (in this case of using language) that we look for to judge that learning has taken place. When pupils play they become absorbed within the imagined world and learn the rules experientially. This is not to diminish the formal teaching of rules, but the fun of play cultivates an attitude that incorporates exploration and experimentation with engagement and enjoyment – a useful mindset to have in any learning situation.

Using the rules of language

I also think it's important to bear in mind that, at least as far as language is concerned, the rules are there to serve the user's purposes: they are a support and should never be a cage. They should guide rather than rigidly prescribe. If we consider that one useful definition of creativity is *going beyond the given*, then the intention to push the rules to see (a) how they work and (b) what lies beyond them is to be encouraged. I've already suggested that play helps to establish the rules, but synergistically an increasing familiarity with the rules acts as a solid platform as pupils reach towards new levels of insight and understanding.

The following activities help to clarify these points to young writers. You can find further resources in the creative wordplay section of my book *Jumpstart! Creativity*.

Answers to pupil activities

Answers to 'Pundemonium' puzzles: sandemonium, gandermonium, candemonium, mandemonium, flandemonium.

Pundemonium

This is a spin on the word *Pandemonium*, which was invented by the poet John Milton (1608–1674) as the capital city of hell in his massive poem 'Paradise Lost'. In other words Pandemonium is a nasty evil place, but *Pundemonium* is just the opposite. It's the place where we'll play with words to get us in the mood to try making poems later. Here are some games that I've had fun with. Pick whichever ones you want to try and, when you've had enough, jump over to another game or move on to the next block of modules.

What is a pun?

A *pun* is a play on words. That means it deliberately uses the fact that a word can mean two or more different things, or that people can mix up similar-sounding words. So, for instance, did you hear about the cross-eyed teacher who couldn't control her pupils? That's an old one. Did you get it? 'Pupils' can mean the pupils (black spots) of your eye and also the kids in a class . . . But explaining it sort of takes the fun out of it, don't you think? Here are some more puns about school:

▶ Trying to write with a broken pencil is pointless.

▶ When there was a power cut at school the other day the kids were de-lighted.

▶ A tiny kid went up to the counter to pay for his school lunch, but he was a little short.

▶ Sometimes my maths teacher is in a good mood and sometimes a bad mood. It just doesn't add up.

▶ A kid in my class accidentally swallowed his dinner money and was rushed to the medical room. Later on I asked the first aid lady about him and she said 'No change yet'.

▶ I wondered why the football seemed to be getting bigger. And then it hit me.

Activities: 'Moniums'

OK, your turn. If Fundemonium is a place where you have fun, and Pundemonium is a place where you make up puns, what do you do in the following places?

▶ Sundemonium

▶ Rundemonium

▶ Wondermonium

▶ Blundermonium

▶ Thundermonium

And what kind of 'monium' do you find if you want to:

▶ play in the sand

▶ look for a male goose

▶ find some empty tins to recycle

▶ go to a place where there are no women

▶ eat an egg custard or crème caramel?

(Ask your teacher for the answers if you need them.)

Here's a similar kind of game. Some time ago a politician invented the phrase 'not fit for purpose' (it was John Reid describing the British immigration system if you must know). By playing about with the words 'fit' and 'purpose' we can make some new puns:

▶ Did you hear about the Sumo wrestler who couldn't put on enough weight to fight and so was not fat for purpose?

▶ Did you hear about the kid who deliberately hid the box of matches at his little brother's birthday party and so the candles were not lit on purpose?

▶ And then there were all the stones left on the bottom of the dolphin's tank at the ocean centre, so it was not flat for porpoise.

Activity: *Create-a-pun*

Now you make up a sentence to explain each of the following:

► not felt for papoose (a papoose is an Algonquian word meaning 'child')

► not hit for her purse

► not wit for more verse.

Using proverbs

Another good way of getting ideas for puns is to look at proverbs. A proverb is supposed to be a short, wise saying. Here's one – You can lead a horse to water but you cannot make him drink. And here's a twist on the idea – You can lead a hearse to water but you cannot make it sink. By 'tweaking' the proverb like this I've made up a new idea for a story or poem.

Here are a few more proverbs-with-twists. Make up a little story to explain each of the puns:

► A third in the band is worth two in the rush (instead of 'A bird in the hand is worth two in the bush').

► A mule and his Tony are soon parted (instead of 'A fool and his money are soon parted').

► In for a pony, in for a sound (instead of 'In for a penny, in for a pound').

If you're in a punny mood, look up some more proverbs and see if you can twist them in this way.

Module 27

Spoonerisms

(There are no teacher's notes for this module.)

A slightly different kind of word-twisting is known as a spoonerism. This is where bits of words and word-sounds change places so that instead of saying 'a ham sandwich' it comes out as 'a sand hamwich' or even 'a sam handwich' or *even* 'a wham handswitch'. The idea comes from the name of the man who made them famous, Dr Archibald Spooner (1844–1930). Dr Spooner apparently made these kinds of slips-of-the-tongue (or tips-of-the-slung) often by accident, but lots of people make up spoonerisms on purpose. It's a good game for keeping your mind nimble, giving yourself a giggle and having new ideas to write about.

Any spoonerism can be fun, but ones that actually make some kind of sense are the best of all. And so 'keys and parrots' (instead of 'peas and carrots') is a better spoonerism than 'a tup of key' (instead of 'a cup of tea').

Here are some well-known spoonerisms:

▶ fighting a liar (lighting a fire)

▶ I searched every crook and nanny (I searched every nook and cranny)

▶ cattle ships and bruisers (battle ships and cruisers)

▶ nosy little cook (cosy little nook)

▶ you've tasted two worms (you've wasted two terms)

▶ a half-warmed fish (a half-formed wish)

▶ is bean dizzy? (is Dean busy?)

Activity: *Creating spoonerisms*

Do you see how a good spoonerism suggests a scene or a little story? Here are a few phrases for you to turn into spoonerisms: 'As we waited to cross the road we watched the *green man*' / 'The salesman was as *keen as mustard*' / 'On the way we saw a *tanned boy*'.

What – nonsense?

Nonsense words have no clear or predefined meaning, although they often carry a certain sense insofar as they can obey the rules of grammar and syntax. So although we might not know what 'smatterised' means we can work out from the -ed ending that it is a past tense verb, while the association with the word 'smattering' (a slight knowledge of, e.g. a language) suggests something made less, perhaps messily given the resonance with the word 'splatter'. So perhaps to be smatterised means to be reduced messily to a state of little understanding? If that makes sense . . .

Useful classroom tips

Using nonsense words with pupils cultivates the sense of exploration and playfulness that I have been trying to emphasise. Especially useful is the fact that, if as teachers we don't know what words mean, we are in the same position as the pupils and must engage in the same process of wordplay. This alone gives us insights into how youngsters must sometimes feel when confronted with baffling ideas in their lessons! And here are some reasons playing with nonsense words can be even more useful:

▶ Helps pupils to feel comfortable and even confident in the presence of uncertainty and ambiguity.

▶ Encourages a search for meaning through picking out context clues. Because words and their meanings are context-dependent, finding and recognising such clues provide insight as to the meaning of 'sensical' words. This can be a useful analytical tool when looking at unfamiliar words in any poem.

▶ Highlights rules of grammar and syntax as pupils endeavour to make sense of letter and word patterns, the -ed ending of smatterised being one example.

▶ Leads pupils, in playing with meanings, to question them. Language manipulates and deceives people every day. It can be powerfully persuasive. Actively engaging with words to seek out their meaning can evolve into an insistence on clarity and precision in the use of language and a tendency not to be impressed or cowed by rhetoric, jargon (especially the pseudo-jargon of politics and advertising) or 'high-flown style'. This seems to be an increasingly necessary skill. Take just one example from the website of the Plain English

Campaign: 'The hours of non-hours work worked by a worker in a pay reference period shall be the total of the number of hours spent by him during the pay reference period in carrying out the duties required of him under his contract to do non-hours work' (from the Department of Trade and Industry's draft law for the minimum wage).

► Serves as an introduction to the poetry of Lewis Carroll and Edward Lear.

Useful websites

www.nonsensicon.com/
www.worldwidewords.org/weirdwords/

What – nonsense?

Nonsense words are great to play with because you don't have to worry about being wrong! You can simply have fun with them as you come to learn more about how 'real' words work. Here are a few games that show you what I mean.

Activity: Criss-cross words

Take two words and make a new word out of them, then suggest a meaning. So for example:

▶ **Puzzle/baffle – to puffle** (verb). It means to confuse someone so much their brains feel like fluff.

▶ **Drink/eat – a dreat** (noun). This is something a bit like ice cream that you can eat and drink at the same time. It's also a bit of a treat. 'To dreat' (verb) means to drink and eat a dreat.

▶ **Boomerang/rattle – a boomerattle** (noun). It's a rattle for babies, and no matter how often they drop it, it will always fly back into their buggy.

▶ **Tip-toe/tinkle – to tiptinkle** (verb) means to walk very carefully through a lot of delicate objects, like bluebells, brittle glass ornaments and so on. 'Tiptinkly' can be used as an adjective. So 'Steve was in a tiptinkly mood' means I'm in trouble with my wife and trying not to say anything that will make the situation worse. A similar expression is 'walking on eggshells' (or in a minefield).

Activity: New inventions

Use word-mixes to think of new inventions that you can write about in stories or poems. Here are some that I created for an inventor called Professor Tom Taylor:

▶ **An airpen**. As you write in the air the pen releases a special kind of smoke that makes letters visible for minutes on end.

▶ **Spray-on carpet**. This does just what it says on the aerosol can. It comes in all sorts of colours. Professor Taylor is working on a patterned version.

▶ **Rubbots**. These are rubber-coated robots. If you make them ball-shaped you can play football by yourself. Or they can be turned into workers who build skyscrapers. If they fall off, no worries because they bounce.

▶ **Hairial**. This is a wig or a hair extension that can pick up your favourite radio or TV station. Use it with an earpiece and special TV glasses (but not in lessons).

What do you think the following inventions do?

▶ sonic glue

▶ liquid light

▶ obedient smoke

▶ a doomerang.

Activity: *What nonsense!*

Finally, have a look at these nonsense words and talk with your classmates about what they might mean:

▶ glombous

▶ snoodled

▶ churdling

▶ squeshy

▶ opticus

▶ direful.

Afterwards, read my poem 'Something Comes By' (www.routledge.com/professional/9780415477529) and see if your ideas fit.

Now that we've got what I call the foundations of writing poetry laid, we have something solid to stand on as we put together the main building blocks. Look at the flowchart to choose your next module.

Am I aloud?

Encouraging reading aloud

Encouraging the pupils to read their own and others' poetry out loud boosts self-confidence and develops communication skills, including listening skills among the audience. A further benefit is that, in order to read from text accurately, pupils need to pay attention to punctuation and other guidance (in the case of poetry such as line breaks and the positioning of words on the white space of the paper). In my opinion well-read poetry reveals its meanings more immediately than if one pores silently over the poem on the page: a poem that's heard is more easily understood, while the beauty and elegance of the language are brought more fully to the fore.

I have come across very little formal or systematic tuition in reading aloud in schools and received none myself while in teacher training. I think this is a great shame and a missed opportunity. Control over the various elements of the voice is an acquired skill that brings many benefits, not just in this context but in other areas of life.

Exploring submodalities

The 'sensory mode' of hearing (the auditory mode) can be split into various components or submodalities. These are:

▶ location (direction and distance)

▶ loudness/softness (soft or harsh)

▶ speed or tempo

▶ continuity (staccato or 'smooth')

▶ rhythm (patterned or unpatterned)

▶ pitch (high or low)

▶ tone (bass or treble)

▶ emotional tone.

It must be said at the outset that trying to think about all of these as one reads is impossible. Once again, the best way to learn how to use the voice *is to use the voice*, gaining experience simply by reading poems aloud. As pupils become more

capable at doing this, further elements of reading to an audience can be included, such as facial expression, eye contact, gesturing and body language.

Useful classroom tips

Initially, however, a few basic guidelines will be enough. I think that in the first instance pupils should:

▶ Familiarise themselves with the poem. If it's their own work they will already know what it means, i.e. how to interpret it. Having said that, it won't do any harm to look over their work with them at the review stage and ask any pertinent questions about word choice, layout etc. If they are reading somebody else's poem make sure they've thought about it: checked unfamiliar words in the dictionary, noted punctuation and line breaks, checked pronunciations.

▶ Rehearse the reading, again with your guidance as necessary. I well remember a pupil being asked to read a story in assembly, in front of the whole school! Both she and the teacher were rightly proud of this excellent piece of work, though we were all mystified by references to the main character's 'oinx pendant'. It was only later I saw that the girl had written 'oynx' but actually meant onyx. Luckily no one in the audience mentioned it at the time, though the poor pupil was still hugely embarrassed afterwards by this mistake.

▶ Learn from you. Please read poetry regularly to the class. Do it simply for the enjoyment of the experience (for them and you) and later discuss the particular inflexions you built into the reading. Have the poem displayed as you read it so that the pupils can match the aural experience with the way the words are laid out visually.

Module
25

FOR THE PUPIL

Am I aloud?

The title of this module is a (bad) pun. Can you see why? Anyway, it's about speaking out loud as you create your poems and when you perform them. The other modules in this block are all about how words and sentences sound, and I think you'll learn a lot faster if you're prepared to say things aloud and not be embarrassed by that.

Tongue twisters

Let's start to practise with some tongue twisters:

▶ You've already met my character Professor Tom Taylor. Well, his children are called Tim and Tina Taylor, and their Mum is named Tanya.

Say this:

Tim and Tina and Tom and Tanya Taylor go out for tea together sometimes for a treat.

Can you say it three times, getting faster each time? I don't know about tongue twister but it's certainly a brain twister!

Here are some well-known tongue twisters. Have a go:

▶ Red lorry, yellow lorry.

▶ Peter Piper picked a peck of pickled peppers.

Did Peter Piper pick a peck of pickled peppers?

If Peter Piper picked a peck of pickled peppers,

where's the peck of pickled peppers Peter Piper picked?

Note: Whether you can say this or not, you might want to find out what a 'peck' is.

▶ Six thick thistle sticks. Six thick thistle sticks.

▶ I slit the sheet, the sheet I slit, and on the slitted sheet I sit (Say this one *very* carefully).

▶ Three free throws.

▶ Unique New York.

Module 25

Practise reading aloud

I believe that the more you practise reading aloud the better you'll become at it. If you want to have a try right now go to our website at www.routledge.com/ professional/9780415477529 and read the poems 'Tucked Up Tight' and 'Listen'.

Take it further

OK, it's time to move on to the next module of your choice . . .

You'll quiver to think that this module is done
And the Reader, excited at last,
Went bounding along on the cheeks of their bum
For this lesson is nearly past.

Syllables and stress

Understanding syllables

A syllable is a 'unit of pronunciation' that forms a word or part of a word and that contains a vowel sound. The idea is easy for pupils to understand as you get them to clap out the syllabic structure of words in a sentence. Such patterns emerge out of the natural cadences – highs and lows, lightness and heaviness – of the human voice. We can immediately notice how the words yesterday, today, tomorrow, for example, are constituted in terms of their separate syllables: yes-ter-day, to-day, to-morr-ow. From there it's a short step to identifying how particular syllables in each word naturally have more weight or emphasis placed upon them as they're spoken – YESterday, toDAY, toMORRow.

In other words, when we speak we naturally stress some syllables while leaving others unstressed. This tendency is exploited to create the musicality, combined with the order and structure of the language, that makes up the aspect of poetry known as *metre* (which is the 'measure' of the spoken lines).

Tone

While stress and tone are interlinked, they are not the same. The tone of the sentence 'I love you', for example, would (presumably) be loving and gentle, and the stress falls on the word 'love'. We say it 'i LOVE you'. If the pupils are not too embarrassed about it, get them to say the sentence and place the emphasis elsewhere. Point out how this changes the meaning of the words: i LOVE you – as opposed to feeling another emotion for you / I love you – regardless of who else might love you / i love YOU – as opposed to me loving someone else. Now ask them to say the sentence naturally, but using different emotional tones. Say 'I love you' in a bored way, or in a sarcastic way, or in a hateful, angry way. This begins to raise pupils' awareness of how stress and tone are blended in speech and highlights again the value of poetry that is spoken aloud and listened to.

Syllables and stress

Before we get started, I'm not talking about stress as in 'stressed out' or feeling tense. Just stay cool while we deal with syllables first . . .

What is a syllable?

A syllable is a bit or a unit of sound that usually includes a vowel sound (check with your teacher about vowels if you've forgotten.) So the word *book* is made up of one syllable. *Paper* has two syllables (pa-per). *Paperback* has three syllables (pa-per-back). You can make this even clearer by clapping out the syllables – book (one clap), paper (two claps), paperback (three claps).

Now look at the word *paperback* more closely. The three syllables are pay-per-back. That's not how you spell the word but how you say it. Notice how you probably say the first syllable with a bit more 'weight' on it, like this – PAY-per-back. It's not likely you say it pay-PER-back or pay-per-BACK. To me they sound a bit strange. This 'weight' that we're talking about is called *stress*. Another term for to 'stress' a sound is to 'emphasise' it.

Activity: Stressing words

We do this all the time as we speak; it's natural. But in poetry we can arrange words so that the stresses (or where we put the weight) make a pattern. Read this – I skipped along the pavement all the way. Did you spot the pattern in that line? It goes – i SKIPPed alONG the PAVEment ALL the WAY. Try putting 'road' instead of 'pavement' and you'll see how that breaks the rhythm of the line. Notice too how the pattern of 'I skipped along the pavement all the way' has a kind of 'skippy' pattern to it. What about – The swirling, the flowing, the tumbling stream?

There are endless patterns that you can create, which is part of the fun of making poems. If you want to learn a bit more about patterns right now, skip along the pavement all the way to **Rhythm (Module 23)**.

Rhythm

The origins of rhythm

Rhythm comes from the Greek *rhythmos* from *rhein* – to flow, which also gives rise to 'stream'. According to the *Longman Dictionary of Word Origins*, 'rhyme' probably sprang from the same root. The essence of rhythm is its musicality combined with its regularity of patterning, although such regularity may be more or less 'strict' depending on the poet's purposes.

Metre

The study and application of rhythmical patterns in poetry are called metre – 'measured' patterns of stressed and unstressed (or 'accented' and 'unaccented') syllables. A pattern of connected syllables is called a metrical 'foot', which, according to the poet Doris Corti, may be because metre establishes measured steps throughout a poem. The metre of the poem is the number of feet to a line.

Using rhythm in poetry

Describing the rhythm (metrical pattern) of a poem, usually by counting and marking out the stressed and unstressed syllables, is called *scansion*. Scanning a poem gives insight into this aspect of the way that it has been constructed and thus forms an important element of pupils' understanding of poetry.

Working through an example

Traditionally, stresses are marked (/) and unstressed syllables (^), so scanning the line in **Syllables and stress (Module 24)** would give us:

```
^   /   ^ /  ^   /    ^  / ^   /
I skipped along the pavement all the way.
```

This makes the metrical pattern of the line very clear. It's a matter of your judgement whether you use the usual symbols for scansion with the pupils, but I think the sooner they become familiar with them the better.

In English, there are four major feet (patterns of stress-no stress). These are:

▶ The iambic foot or iamb. This is an unstressed syllable followed by a stressed one (^ /):

```
   ^  /
Today
```

Module **23**

▶ The trochaic foot or trochee. This is a stressed syllable followed by an unstressed one (/ ^):

/ ^
Calling

▶ The anapaestic foot or anapaest. This is two unstressed syllables followed by a stressed one (^ ^ /):

^   ^   /
Underneath

▶ The dactylic foot or dactyl. This is a stressed syllable followed by two unstressed (/ ^ ^):

/ ^   ^
Yesterday

We can now see that 'I skipped along the pavement all the way' is made up of five iambic feet:

1   2   3   4   5
^   /   ^ /   ^   /   ^   /   ^   /
I skipped along the pavement all the way.

There are traditional names for the numbers of feet in a line. These are: one foot – monometer; two feet – dimeter; three feet – trimeter; four feet – tetrameter; five feet – pentameter; six feet – hexameter; seven feet – heptameter; eight feet – octometer.

So, because our line is made up of five iambic feet it is said to be written in *iambic pentameter*. This is one of the most common and familiar metrical patterns in English verse.

Useful classroom tips

Although these ideas are basic to the study of metre, they do come bundled up with a crop of difficult words, which some pupils might find daunting. Again it's a matter of your professional judgement as to if, how and when you introduce these terms. My instinct would be simply to let pupils listen to a variety of metrical patterns that they can then copy and play with as they experiment with their own words and rhythms.

If you want to know more about metre (and there's plenty more to know!), I would recommend Doris Corti's *Writing Poetry* and *The Complete Idiot's Guide to Writing Poetry* by Nikki Moustaki.

Rhythm

What is rhythm?

The word rhythm means 'to flow', and it's the way the voice rises and falls as lines of poetry are spoken. Having said that, while some poems have a very strong and regular rhythm, others have 'looser' or freer rhythms, and some have no rhythm at all. In other words, rhythm is one of the building blocks of poetry that you can choose to use or not.

Using rhythm

Say these lines out loud:

▶ Bubble, bubble, toil and trouble.

▶ I once met a girl from Skegness.

▶ When forty winters shall besiege thy brow.

▶ It never looks like summer here / On Beeny by the sea.

▶ If I were James Bond for a day.

Can you spot the rhythm or the 'beat' that goes on in these lines? If you repeat a line three or four times you might find that the rhythm is clearer. Try clapping to a line also. Put this mark, /, above the part of the word (the syllable) where you feel you want to clap.

For the first line, this is how I want to clap it:

```
   /      /     /       /
Bubble, bubble, toil and trouble.
```

You can see that the line has a nice regular rhythm. Now add this mark, ^, above the syllables where you don't clap. Now the line looks like this:

```
 /  ^  /  ^  /  ^   /  ^
Bubble, bubble, toil and trouble.
```

In other words, the line is made up of four of these: / ^. Where the 'claps' go in a line of poetry, and how many times the pattern is repeated are called the metre (or measure) of the verse. Your teacher may want to tell you more about this.

I don't think it's necessary for you to know very much about the 'rules' of rhythm to write your own poems (other people might disagree). I think it's more important that you enjoy the rhythm when you listen to other people's poems and maybe have a go at using it in your own work. If you've clapped out the other lines we used as examples of rhythm, try marking out the pattern of them now using the / and ^ signs.

You'll realise that rhythm is something else that's to do with the way a poem *sounds* when it's spoken. To learn more about sound, bubble over to the next module, **Alliteration and friends** (**Module 22**).

By the way, what would *you* do if you were James Bond for a day? Maybe you'll write a poem about it. I did, and if you want to read it go to www.routledge.com/professional/9780415477529.

Alliteration and friends

Alliteration refresher

Alliteration is a common linguistic/literary device that, along with assonance and onomatopoeia, composes the 'sonic three' techniques that pupils are encouraged to use in their work – poetry and prose. Rather than going over old ground now I'll just make a few brief points that you might find useful:

▶ There is a difference between alliteration and 'consonance'. Alliteration is the repetition of *initial* consonant sounds (*brown bears bother badgers boisterously*), while consonance is the repetition of consonant sounds within words (ro*tt*en bo*tt*les sha*tt*er ra*ttl*es).

▶ Euphony and cacophony are useful ideas when encouraging the pupils to play with sounds. Euphony is when the flow of words in a story or poem is smooth and pleasing, while cacophony is produced when words create a harsh, jagged, grating effect. So Tennyson's famous line is euphonic – *The murmuring of innumerable bees*. Whereas Gerard Manley Hopkins' line is cacophonous – *The blood-gush blade-gash* (quoted in Moustaki). Of course the effect in both cases is deliberate, designed to suit the subject matter of the poem. A useful activity to do with the pupils is to help them make a word web on the topic of, say, a summer's day, a stream etc. and one for a building site or busy kitchen (these two look the same in our house). Once you have plenty of words to work with, ask the pupils to create a 'sound FX' sheet (see **Sound FX (Module 35)**) for each, or even a poem that may include some rhythm.

▶ Standard advice to adult writers is to be careful not to overuse these devices. With pupils I feel it's different. Excessive use will probably be part of their emergent understanding as they learn. I well remember explaining apostrophes to classes, only to have the pupils' work 'measled' with apostrophes for days or weeks afterwards, until they learned to use them accurately and with a more delicate touch.

FOR THE TEACHER

Useful classroom tips

One activity that works well is to suggest a simple list poem based on close observation (perhaps from memory) of a particular place. This focus can produce some great results, such as James Trinder's poem, which I'm sure you'll agree is full of 'busyness' and exuberance. James is six by the way – and how I wish I'd thought of that brilliant title.

Building Sight!

Engines growling.
Dumpers dumping.
Plant reversing.
Lights flashing.
Spirit levels making sure things are flat.
Foremen planning.
Builders building.
Trowels slapping.
Spades throwing
Soil in a pile.
Boulders in a heap.
Fork lift trucks.
Walls all around me.
My view is almost . . . gone!

Alliteration and friends

Using alliteration

You have probably done some work on alliteration in class already, and assonance and onomatopoeia too. This takes us back to consonants and vowels. Remember:

▶ Alliteration means repeating consonant sounds at the start of words. *Peter Piper picked a peck of pickled peppers* is a good example with all of those repeated Ps.

Assonance

The vowels are **a**, **e**, **i**, **o** and **u** (sometimes the letter **y** is counted too). Assonance means repeating vowel *sounds* in a phrase or sentence. Note 'sounds', because any vowel can make different sounds. For instance, the letter 'a' sounds different in 'cat' and 'cart', or 'fat' and . . . I know what you're thinking. I was going to say 'father'. Can you think of other examples using different vowels?

Onomatopoeia

Onomatopoeia happens when the sound that a word makes as you say it is the same as the meaning of that word. Really easy examples are bang, splash, clang, tinkle, whoosh. Here are a few sentences that use the sound effects we've talked about:

▶ The fly flew buzzing and whizzing around.

▶ Steve slipped trudging through mud, wellies slurping, sloshing and sucking in the muck.

▶ Fire snapped and crackled, kindling the twigs alight with a whoosh and gush of flames.

Activity: Using onomatopoeia

Have a go at making up a few more examples of your own. A good way is to imagine a scene like a busy playground, cooks preparing meals in the kitchen of a packed restaurant, people at a swimming pool etc. Then talk with your friends about the sounds you would hear and gather them up (the sounds, not your friends) into a 'sonic sentence'.

Activity: *Using sound effects*

If you're up for the challenge you might have a go at making some poems or at least short verses using the sound effects you've learned about. They can be as short and simple as this traditional rhyme:

> Knock at the knocker,
> Ring at the bell,
> Give us a copper
> For singing so well.

This is what carol singers would chorus after they'd finished their Christmas carols outside someone's house. A 'copper' by the way is a penny, not a policeman.

Take it further

And if you want to read a longer poem that uses rhythm and sound effects brilliantly, try 'Night Mail' by W. H. Auden.

> And now I think we have to go
> Because, you see, it's time –
> So hurry children don't be slow –
> Let's find out more on rhyme.

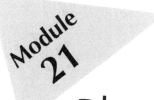

Rhyme

To rhyme, or not to rhyme?

One of the best known of the 'classic' books on teaching pupils about poetry is Sandy Brownjohn's *Does It Have To Rhyme?* Well of course it doesn't, although pupils undoubtedly enjoy rhyming poetry, both listening to it and striving towards it for themselves. One danger of suggesting to young writers that a poem must, should or can rhyme is that, if they go for it, the sense gets lost in the process. How often have we read through a pupil's poem only to find that they've got those end words to match, but what the hell does it all mean?

I think we must again invoke the argument of emergent understanding. Often, when it's suggested to pupils that they can use rhyme, it's like a new bike: they ride it endlessly and sometimes recklessly, wobble and fall, but eventually get the hang of it. Then the riding has a certain ease and assurance about it that indicates experience. So it is with rhyme (though I would hesitate in setting pupils the task of writing a poem featuring both rhyme and apostrophes!).

Even relatively little practice can yield impressive results. This is from Daniel Netherwood, eight years old:

A Winter's Day

I went out today to see the frosty trees
Slippery ice like glassy seas
The jagged cold and frosty snow
Icicle daggers hanging low
The frosty landscape cold and white
Slippery ice crystals clear and bright
Crunchy snow beneath my feet
Chilling winds taking all the heat
The frosty mountains way up high
All these things I saw as I walked by.

FOR THE TEACHER

Useful classroom tips

But even at the outset in 'teaching' rhyme – if that's the right word – we might offer the ancient piece of Oriental advice that pupils should use it as one would cook a small fish: lightly.

Another way of tackling the issue is to use the overkill strategy. Make pupils think of rhymes until they're totally fed up with the whole idea, then switch to something completely different. When you return to looking at the subject, the pupils might be far more discerning and use rhyme more thoughtfully and delicately. And, I might suggest, avoid rhyming dictionaries like the plague. This is likely to tear the living heart out of the creative process, as the pupils' energy will be diverted to flipping through pages looking for 'good rhymes' rather than writing what they feel.

Rhyme

> Roses are red,
> Violets are blue.
> Some poems rhyme
> And others don't.

Yes, I know, not very funny, but it's good advice all the same. Rhyme – which means a matching of sounds – is a part of poetry that you use *if it helps you to make a better poem*. And even then, if you decide to use it, you don't *have* to use it all the way through. Use it when you think it's needed.

Facts about rhyme

In the next block of modules you'll have the chance to play with rhymes as you look at different sorts of poems. Before we move on, here are a few more basic facts about rhyme:

▶ Straight rhyme means words that rhyme exactly – walk/talk, faces/laces. Think of a few more rhyming pairs, just to get the hang (sang/clang) of it.

▶ Slant rhyme or half rhyme is where words sound similar but don't rhyme exactly – short/hurt/that, heaven/even/given. Again, see if you can come up with groups-of-three slant rhymes.

▶ Internal or inside rhyme. Here words within the line can rhyme, sometimes with words at the end of the line. A few examples are:

  – The moon shone white right through the night.

  – And the still misty cloud draped the hills like a shroud.

  – So please to remember the fifth of November.

Something I would like you to look at now is comparisons. So after you've read the brilliant and wonderful poem below, move on to the next module.

> Roses are red,
> Violets are blue,
> Some poems don't rhyme
> While others do.

Comparisons

Everyday metaphor

Metaphor is fundamental to the way we use language. In fact, metaphor is so widespread and ingrained even in mundane, day-to-day speech that often we barely notice it and most certainly take it for granted. What are the metaphors in the following short conversation for example?

ELSIE: You've got some lovely sunflowers springing up in your garden Doris.

DORIS: Yes they are nice. But they do attract the ladybirds. On hot days the flowers are smothered with them!

ELSIE: I love the way the flowers all face the sun. Mind you, that lawn is carpeted with daisies. They shoot up everywhere, don't they?

DORIS: (looking skywards) Right enough. It's glorious today – not like last Saturday. I was out here weeding and the sun was cruel, I can tell you. Roasting hot it was, like being in an oven.

No doubt you'll have spotted plenty of comparisons – though perhaps not 'sunflowers', 'ladybirds' or 'glorious'. It's a salutary lesson to write down snippets of ordinary conversation and note how much we rely on metaphor and other representational devices. Although, having said that, *all* language is representational, since words stand for things and are not the things themselves. As someone rightly said, one can die of hunger if all you've got is the menu.

The advantage of using metaphor

The advantage of metaphor being so ingrained in the language means that pupils already use it very naturally. Their challenge is to bring freshness and individuality to their comparisons and so, as far as they can, avoid clichés. Clichés are seductive because they're easy: they can be lifted 'off the peg' (there I just did it) and dropped wholesale (oops, another one) into a poem; and also because, if we pay closer attention to them, an echo of their original power can be detected. As Fred Sedgwick in *Teaching Poetry* comments, many clichés were originally striking pieces of imagery. He quotes the example of a rumour or panic 'spreading like wildfire'. Simply visualising how such a fire must look revitalises the force of the comparison. In this case too, while the use of 'like' makes the comparison a simile, the word 'wildfire' is itself a metaphor – the way fire looks and moves 'as though it were wild'. The ferocity, strength and speed implied here are striking, while that recognition gives us an insight into a metaphor-making activity . . .

From 'wildfire' we can leap to the 'tamefire' of coals glowing cosily in the grate. And how about 'lionfire', 'tigerfire' or 'wolf-fire' (though this last is a bit clumsy and I think would sound better as 'wolfenfire'). What image does 'eaglefire' conjure in your mind? Make up a few more for yourself and encourage the pupils to do so too, along with some of the other comparison games in their module.

Note: There are more activities in my companion volume *Countdown to Creative Writing*.

Comparisons

All of us use comparisons every day. Not long ago I had a bad cold and as I sat hunched on the sofa with a blanket around me my wife said 'You look like death warmed up!' That didn't make me feel any better, but afterwards I did think about what a good comparison it was. One way of thinking about 'death' is to imagine the Grim Reaper – that terrifying hooded skeleton figure. So I looked like that! But also someone who's dead is pale and still and, um, doesn't look very well. But I was also like death 'warmed up', so I was moving about a bit and had a touch of colour. At least that's what I think 'warmed up' means here. So my imagination had to do some work on that – and it's always a good thing when your imagination has to do some work.

So comparisons are everywhere. They're as common as muck (or, if you don't want to be quite so crude about it, as common as poo-poo). Or as common as the stars in the sky, or sand grains on the beach or . . . But maybe you'll think of some better ones now.

Why compare?

Comparisons are used in poetry because they make the reader's imagination do a lot by using a small number of words. And that's one important quality of poetry: it's a condensed kind of writing.

Simile, metaphor and personification

You'll often come across three types of comparison. These are simile, metaphor and personification. You might have studied these before, but if not – and briefly:

▶ A simile compares things using words such as 'like' or 'as' or 'seemed'.

> I flash through your mind
> Like a shooting star
> Or linger ghost-like in your head.
> (from 'Ideas') (www.routledge.com/professional/9780415477529)

▶ A metaphor leaves out 'like' and 'as' and compares things directly, as in the line 'lakes brightly mirror the heaven's blue' (from 'Weathers'). (www.routledge.com/professional/9780415477529). Here, the appearance of the lake is being compared to the shiny reflections you get in a mirror.

▶ Personification is comparing what's not human with a person or some aspect of a person, such as a part of the body or an emotion. In my poem 'Tharsis' I call the wind mad and compare it to a howling savage (www.routledge.com/professional/9780415477529). Notice how that comparison goes through the entire poem.

Handy hints for comparison

Learning to use comparisons well (and rhyme, rhythm and many other elements of poetry) is a matter of experience. But there are two things you should remember from the outset:

1   Don't overdo it. It's easy to overload a poem with comparisons, so once you've written it go back over it to check that.

2   Don't mix metaphors. That means don't use two different comparisons close together when you are talking about one thing. 'In pulling the cat out of the bag he threw the baby away with the bathwater'. That's a mixed metaphor.

Take it further

▶ If you'd like to play some comparison games – read on.

▶ If you've had enough and want to think about the way your poem will look on the page, go to **What's the point?** (**Module 19**).

▶ If you're really keen and want to try writing some simple poems, go to the next block of modules (check the flowchart).

Activity: Simple similes

As snug as a bug in a rug. That's a simile and quite a catchy one too because of the rhyme. Can you make up a few more? Here are some I thought of:

▶ As fat as a cat on the mat.

▶ As free as a bee out to sea.

▶ As remote as a goat in a boat.

The third one isn't as good as the others I think, because *why* would a goat in a boat be remote? He could just as well be close by. The best similes of this kind make sense straight away. So although I could say 'as light as a mite on a kite' it's not as immediate and so not as good as 'as free as a bee out to sea'.

Here's another simile – he ran like the wind. Usually when we say that we mean he ran quickly, although when you think about it the wind can be very gentle and slow. But anyway, if we wanted to describe somebody running quickly in another way we could say 'he ran like lightning'. Can you think of a few more ways of describing somebody running quickly? Use 'like' or 'as' – he ran as fast as lightning.

Now make up a few more examples for each of these:

▶ He was as happy as a pig in mud.

▶ She was as pretty as a picture.

▶ It fell like a stone.

▶ The rumour spread like wildfire.

Activity: Criss cross comparisons

Take a look at Table 3. We're going to make some comparisons between the weather and animals. All you have to do is pick an animal, then pick a kind of weather and put them together. (**Tip**: try using dice like you did in **Motivation** (**Module 38**), to choose them at random. You might come up with some unusual ideas!)

Table 3

	Storm	Sunshine	Ice/snow	Lightning	Hurricane	Fog
Cat						
Wolf						
Eagle						
Elephant						
Shark						
Butterfly						

You can play this game in different ways. When you've picked an animal plus weather, try working the comparison both ways:

The cat pounced like lightning or *The lightning clawed at the sky*.

Notice in that second one I used the idea of the cat to think of 'clawed'. If I chose snow + snake I could say *The snow slithered out of the sky on to the wet roofs and pavements*. That verb 'slithered' came to my mind because I was thinking about a snake.

Module 20

When you've thought of a few comparisons, try extending them a little. There's a beautiful poem by Carl Sandburg called 'The Fog' (you'll find it on the Internet). You can use the poem as a model to write something similar of your own. I had a go and came up with this:

> Snowflakes come
> softly, silently like mice.
>
> They twitch whiskers of ice,
> tickling grass and bushes
> and are gone with the first light
> of dawn.

By the way, you can change any of the words in the Table 3 grid to suit yourself.

Activity: *Person power*

A lot of the gods and goddesses in ancient religions are personifications. In Norse (Viking) mythology, for instance, Thor was the god of thunder. In Roman myth, Mars was the god of war. In Greek myth, Helios was the sun god. There are lots of other examples. We've already met the Grim Reaper who personifies death and we've mentioned Jack Frost. Jack Frost comes out of English folklore and was an elvish, mischievous figure who left frosty patterns on glass and icy whiskers on leaves. Some people think he's the same character as Father Winter, who appears in Viking folklore.

Here's a question. If a beautiful, clear, starry night were a person, what would he or she look like? What sort of temperament (moods) would that person have?

Think of a couple more. Pick a scene/landscape/kind of weather and turn it into a person. When you have a character clearly in mind, try describing them in a poem. Use Carl Sandburg's poem as a model, or try some of the other forms of poetry you'll read about in the next block.

Tip: This kind of personification can help you to make up great characters for your stories. If your character is a thief, think fog and darkness. If your character is a beautiful girl, think summer and woodlands. Many metaphors that we use are personifications of this kind – 'she had a sunny personality' / 'he gave her a wintry smile' / 'she returned his icy glare' / 'my memory of the party is rather foggy'.

Now choose your next module and go there on little cat feet.

Module
19

What's the point?

Punctuation and the poem on the page

(There are no teacher's notes for this module.)

What do these two phrases mean? – 'Thirty-odd children' / 'Thirty, odd children'.

Why is the meaning of the following sentence unclear? – 'He took books down from two of his fathers shelves'.

Which version of this line do you think is easier to read?

► Tree tapper grub grabber writhing maggot muncher bright blood red woodland dweller . . .

► Tree tapper, grub grabber, writhing-maggot muncher, bright blood-red woodland dweller . . .

Punctuate!

You don't need me to tell you that punctuation helps our writing to be clearer – your teacher has probably mentioned it loads of times. It's also important in poetry of course. Gerard Manley Hopkins, one of my favourite poets, gave this advice when reading poetry – to let the punctuation guide you. I think that's also very useful when you're writing it. Punctuation marks are like little precision instruments. When you think about which instrument to use and why, it can make what you mean to say much easier to understand.

But having said that, once you know how punctuation works you can play tricks with it. There is a very interesting poet called e e cummings . . . Wait, did you spot that? I didn't use capital letters in his name, and neither did he. I wonder what the reason is for that? He used punctuation in a very unusual way. Find his poem 'Chanson Innocente' on the Internet and notice how the first few lines are set out and punctuated. Why do you think e e cummings decided to do things like that?

How does your poem look?

So another point to consider with poetry is how your poem will look on the page. I'm not talking about neatness, but about where you will place your words on the white background of the paper or computer screen. To help explain this, look again at the poem 'Donna Didn't Come Back' (www.routledge.com/professional/ 9780415477529). Notice how the words are arranged. Would it still be a poem if it looked like this?

> Donna didn't come back on Monday. We all knew what had happened and found we couldn't remember her face before her crutches and fallen-out hair. No one ever talked about what she had or what she was. Even so, and despite her eyes which said I'm tired I give up, we all expected her to come in that door sit down to maths and pretend the world was still OK.

Personally, I think poetry is also about the way the words are set out on the page, and that one important reason for doing this is to guide the reader when speaking the poem out loud.

When you read someone's poem, always assume that everything you see on the page has been done deliberately, for a reason. Ask yourself (and others) questions that search for those reasons; you don't have to know what those reasons are and, in fact, you might never work them out. It's the searching and the asking that are powerful and important.

So with 'Donna Didn't Come Back':

► Why might the first sentence take up two short lines? Why is 'on Monday' dropped down on to the second line?

► Why is 'OK' at the end put on a line by itself?

► Why is the whole poem written with such short lines?

If you found Carl Sandburg's poem 'The Fog' on the Internet, you'll notice that it too is set out in a particular way. What questions could you ask about the layout? What reasons for it occur to you?

FOR THE PUPIL

Shape poems

(There are no teacher's notes for this module.)

Shaping your poem

While we're on the subject of 'poetry on the page', I'll mention *shape poems*. These are poems where the words are arranged to look like the thing they're describing. A simple example is to draw around your hand, then on the palm write 'How useful are hands!' and then along each finger write a short sentence about how hands are useful. One girl in a school I visited made this poem:

> How useful are hands!
> Hammer blows or careful threading
> Clapping, pointing, waving, clasping
> Make a million different things
> Lovers' touch and mother's caring
> Writing, painting, giving, sharing.

Why sculpt a poem?

Shape poems add an extra dimension to your writing. The topic itself suggests how the words would be arranged on the page. It's easy to visualise how a poem about a snake would look for example – Can you see it in your mind's eye right now, even if you don't know what the words are yet? Also the topic can lead you to think about other 'poetical devices': my snake-shape-poem would have plenty of alliteration and assonance, plenty of hissy slithery sliding through the grass. Finally, shape poems are fun because you can fit them into pictures, collage, make mobiles with them (how would a shape poem mobile about the Solar System look?) or even 3D models. If you want more ideas about shape poems do a quick search on the Internet and you'll be spoilt for choice.

Diamante poems

Before we leave this module I'll tell you about diamante poems (die-ah-man-tay). The word 'diamante' comes from diamond and that tells you about their shape. But there's also a clear structure to them that gives you a chance to practise your parts of speech. This is how a diamante poem is put together – see Figure 7.

Note: A diamante poem can be about just one thing as in my first example, or about two contrasting topics. See the poem on Summer–Winter.

Structure of the poem:

Opening topic
Adjective + adjective
3 x ing words
Four nouns or a short phrase
3 x ing words
Adjective + adjective
Closing topic.

First example: single topic.

Cats
playful, aloof
hiding, stalking, pouncing
mice, leaves, butterflies, bees
hissing, meowing, purring
alert, waiting
alive.

Second example: contrasting topics.

Summer
warm, gentle
swimming, sunbathing, ballplaying
the world spins in space
snowballing, skating, huddling
cold, harsh
winter.

Figure 7

Module
18

Once you've got into the swing of diamante poems you'll find that it's easy to write plenty of them. If by any chance you do have difficulty, work with your teacher and classmates to create word webs of the topics that interest you. Out of that brainstorming will come plenty of words you can arrange in the diamond shape.

Other forms of poetry

There are many other forms that poetry can take. The next block of modules looks at some of the simpler ones. Remember that, although your choice of topic may guide you to a particular form, often your theme may be expressed through two or more forms of poetry. I wrote a diamante poem about summer and winter, but it could just as easily be a kenning poem, or a list poem, or a 'what if' poem etc.

Take a look at the next section on the flowchart (page 3) – **First steps** (**Modules 17–7**) – and pick the next module you'd like to visit. I've arranged them from simpler to more complex, but don't let that stop you from jumping in wherever you want.

Alliterative phrases/ kennings

Various researchers and scholars point up the power of alliterative phrases. Seth Lindstromberg and Frank Boers, for instance, emphasise that alliteration is a device extensively used in politics, advertising and the media as well as in literature, giving examples such as 'drive the dream', *Mad Max*, *Pride and Prejudice*, 'life long learning' and others. According to these authors, 13 per cent of idiomatic phrases in modern colloquial English are alliterative (www.hltmag.co.uk/jan05/mart03.htm#C5).

Creating catchy phrases

We say that such phrases are catchy; they 'catch in the memory'. *It takes two to tango* is punchier and more memorable than *It takes a couple to dance*. A useful as well as fun activity to do with the pupils is to have them collect examples of alliterative phrases from magazines, TV and books and 'translate' them into non-alliterative form. The pupils will probably find that the transformed words are somehow less satisfying and enjoyable now. And prompt them to ponder more possibilities – use the phrase *Mad Max* for instance as a springboard for inventing further feature film titles – *Super Simon*, *Crazy Karly*, *Doug the Dodgy Detective*.

Search through proverbs too and you'll soon discover, among many others: 'A bad beginning makes a good ending' / 'A clear conscience is a coat of mail' / 'In for a penny in for a pound' / 'A miss is as good as a mile' / 'A word to the wise is enough'.

The common use of alliteration here is not accidental but may be subliminal; in other words, not conscious and deliberate but arising subconsciously from what we have already called the 'natural cadences' of human speech.

Alliterative phrases

Speaking out loud

We've already come across the idea that poetry (originally anyway) was meant to be spoken and listened to before it was looked at visually on the page. When a poem is spoken, the extra dimension of the human voice is added to the experience. Now that's an obvious thing to say, but the point is important. Think about the different parts of the voice aside from the content, the words themselves. We've got:

Volume	–	loud to quiet
Pitch	–	high to low
Pace or **tempo**	–	fast to slow
Tone	–	the mood or emotion of the voice
Timbre	–	a bundle of 'qualities' that make the voice individual (these will include the ones above).

Different voices

Take a few minutes just to listen to people's voices and notice *how much goes on* when someone speaks. Listen to kids in the playground, the teachers at school, actors on TV. What is it about somebody's voice that makes it easy and enjoyable to listen to or, on the other hand (or lip), what makes a voice really irritating?

The qualities of the voice are important of course whenever you want to read your own poetry out loud. You can explore this further in the document called **Performance poetry** at www.routledge.com/professional/9780415477529.

Soundscapes

For now, let's focus on another element of the 'soundscape' of a poem: the effect of putting certain words together. Perhaps you've already looked at **Alliteration and friends (Module 22)**: I'm talking about the same thing here, but with a special emphasis on sound.

Make the sound 'cr', as in crunch. Say crunch five or six times. 'Crunch crunch crunch crunch crunch'. Did a picture come into your head? My imagination made two pictures, first someone walking quickly over frozen snow and then a child eating cereal (with not much milk).

Have you ever noticed how the 'cr' sound crops up in other words, such as crisp, crackle, crush, crinkle and crumble? Say those words out loud. When I say them my hand wants to clench, as though I'm crushing something crispy or crunchy – and it makes a crackling sound. It's easy then for me to think of a sentence such as 'I kicked my way through the crispy leaves, crushing them down crunch – crunch – crunch'. Well that's a bit over the top but it does emphasise the point.

Finally, notice how often alliteration (and assonance and onomatopoeia) crops up in our everyday language. Examples that come to mind are 'bumblebee', 'busy bee', 'crafty cat', 'sky high', 'Big Ben', 'garden gate', 'super saver', 'bargain bucket' . . . Maybe you'll think of some more to add to the list.

Alliteration has been around for a long time. If you want to learn more about that, tip-toe-tappy-toe over to **Kennings** (**Module 16**).

Kennings

Going back in time

The *kenning* is a very old and interesting way of using words. It goes back at least as far as poetry written by the Vikings and the Celts, probably well over a thousand years ago. The word 'kenning' means 'to name after', which is to say that one thing is named or described as something else. So, for instance, the phrase 'bundle of joy' is an interesting way of describing a baby. But another way of writing it is 'joy-bundle', which is the way kenning-like phrases often look.

Here's a harder example. What am I referring to here?

> Tree tapper, grub grabber, writhing-maggot muncher,
> bright blood-red woodland dweller . . .
>
> Fresh grass-green-leaf hunter,
> spotted soarer, flying fantasy flapping furiously, feathery featured,
> glisten-eyed small-speckled songster . . .

If you worked out it was a woodpecker, well done. If you thought it was a bag of wine-gums, look again.

Do you see how a kenning makes use of another little trick of language that we looked at earlier? I'm talking about alliteration. If you need to refresh your memory about that flip back to **Alliteration and friends** (**Module 22**) or **Alliterative phrases** (**Module 17**).

Kenning checklist

My little woodpecker poem was made up of kennings. Remember, a kenning:

▶ is a metaphor

▶ uses alliteration

▶ may be a riddle.

Notice too how I sometimes use a hyphen (-) to join pairs of words.

Module 16

Activity: *Create a kenning*

If you'd like to have a go at making kennings, take a look at the examples in Table 4 and then try some of your own.

Table 4		
Object	**Kenning**	**Another example**
Fork	Food lifter	Meat piercer
My wife	Bargain hunter	Life partner
Book	Knowledge-giver	
Falcon	Sky-warrior	
The Sun		
iPod		
	Mouse stalker	
	Distance-eater	

Can you put a number of kenning-like phrases together to create a longer description? Describe yourself, for instance, or a fictional character, a machine or a place. Each time you create a kenning it means that you've looked at that object or person in a new way, so it's a useful exercise in strengthening your 'poetical eye' (see **The poetical eye (Module 43)**).

Alien's eye view

Pretend you're an alien exploring Earth. You understand a little of the Earthlings' language but don't know the common names for things, so you wouldn't know a car is called a car for instance. To report back to home planet you have to make up kenning-like descriptions of common objects. Look at their shape and how they move and any other details. Here's how you might describe that car– smoky speed-box, hurrying buzz-buzz road-insect, spinning rubberfoot, busy stinkbug.

Here we have four interesting ways of looking at a car. Try being an alien for a few minutes and see how *different* things can look to you . . .

Three-step game

Writing free verse

This simple technique helps to introduce pupils to *free verse* (see more at **Module 3**). As Doris Corti asserts in *Writing Poetry*, free verse is not merely prose split up into shorter lines. True enough, it has broken away from strict metre and regular rhyme, but the lines of a free verse poem are full of subtle emphases, rhythmical patterns and resonances of sound that can create a beautiful smoothness, a silky flow that carries the listener on.

At its most basic, a 'three-step' consists of three short lines focusing on the chosen topic.

> A crescent moon melts
> quietly
> in the evening sky.

The line breaks are not random. Read the words aloud and you may pick up the 'lilt' and the intended gentle rhythm of the piece. You must use your judgement in deciding whether any pupil's ear is attuned enough to notice it, and whether therefore the pupil can attempt something similar in their own writing.

Anaphora

Another kind of three-step uses a poetical/rhetorical device known as an anaphora (pronounced un-*naf*-er-uh). This is a simple repetition of words and phrases:

> Here is the crescent moon
> Here is the western sky
> Here is the evening calm.

Such repetition can be extended beyond three lines and may be incorporated into the list poems mentioned in **Module 12**. The piece sounds a little rigid and mechanical, and would become more so if it ran to four lines or beyond. Small changes can help to shift the language towards something more fluid:

> Here is the crescent moon
> Here the western sky
> Here an evening calm.

When a line becomes too long in a free verse poem, including a three-step, it is 'folded' under itself to form another line, which is indented to indicate that the meaning continues.

> Here is the crescent moon
> > melting
> > > down the western sky.

Here the arrangement of the words on the page mirrors the progress of the moon as it sinks towards the horizon. If you find that some pupils enjoy the challenging simplicity of the three-step, you might suggest this subtlety to them and encourage 'three-step shape poems' on a chosen theme.

> > > a lamp among the stars.
> > shining,
> Jupiter rising now

This arrangement can be read bottom-up (the original intention) or top-down without losing sense.

Three-step game

This does what it says on the tin. A three-step poem is a very short three-line piece that is often a description. A simple three-step looks like this:

> Black clouds roll across
> the thundery sky
> this dark afternoon.

These three lines describe something big and dramatic. It doesn't have to be like that.

> One whisker,
> the butterfly's tongue,
> tasting sweet nectar.

This describes a very tiny detail. Have you ever watched a butterfly's tongue (called a proboscis) uncurl like one of those whistles you blow at a party? Have you ever looked at the whole movement of the sky on a dark stormy day? We're going right back to the idea of noticing (**Module 41**) in order to have something to say (**Module 39**). Some of the most beautiful and popular poems ever written are based on the things that happen in nature. But you can notice anything you like if you want a topic for a three-step poem.

> The mantelpiece clock
> patiently counts time
> in my hurried life.

Notice that this is just one sentence. Why do you think I might have arranged it into three lines like this? Ask your teacher to help you work it out. Something else you can do to add to a three-step poem is play with the arrangement of the words on the page.

> The mantelpiece clock
> > Patiently – counts – time
> > > inmyhurriedlife.

Why do you think I might have arranged the words like this? Think about it before you read my thoughts:

▶ I put dashes between the words on the second line to suggest the regular ticking of

$$\wedge \quad / \quad \wedge \quad / \quad \wedge \quad /$$
the clock – the way it counts the time.

▶ I stuck all the words in the third line together to suggest hurrying and everything happening quickly.

▶ I shifted each line a bit more to the right to suggest time moving on.

It's absolutely fine to play about with words like this; and the best kind of playing around is when you have a *reason* for what you do.

Activity: *Writing a three-step poem*

Here are a few suggested topics for a three-step poem. Pick one and have a go:

▶ A traffic jam on the motorway.

▶ Waking up on the first morning of your holiday.

▶ A birthday party.

These are simple, ordinary things. I'm sure you can think of many more.

Using repetition is another way of creating a three-step.

> Be patient says the mantelpiece clock.
> Be patient says the swing of the sun.
> Be patient say the circling seasons.

Or

> The mantelpiece clock, ever patient.
> The mantelpiece clock measures time.
> The mantelpiece clock fears not death.

You may have looked at the earlier modules about stress, syllables and rhythm (**Modules 24** and **23**). When you write three-step poems you don't have to be concerned with exactly how many syllables are in each line. In fact, lines can vary in length and number of syllables – although, as you see, the lines tend to be quite short. Nor do you have to stick to a definite rhythm (lines all following a pattern). But if you read the poems out loud you may notice that they have a 'rhythmical feel' to them.

Module
14

Uni-verses

(There are no teacher's notes for this module.)

That's just me trying to be clever. A 'verse' actually means a single line, usually found in poetry. But many people think of it as a number of lines that all talk about the same subject – a bit like a paragraph in a story. Another name for it is a *stanza*. The word stanza means 'stopping place' in Italian. A typical verse or stanza looks like this:

> 'What do you think you're doing?'
> said Miss Casey looking mad.
> 'Nothing Miss,' I answered
> feeling foolish, feeling sad –

By the way, if you want to read the rest of this poem it's called 'Daydreamy' (www.routledge.com/professional/9780415477529).

You'll see that this verse has a rhythm to it and also it rhymes. Many verses are like that. In the verse above, the rhyme happens with 'mad' and 'sad'. The other two end words, 'doing' and 'answered', don't rhyme at all.

You can mark out the rhyme pattern of a verse like this: Give the first end word the code letter a. Any other end words that rhyme with it are coded a too. If the second end word doesn't rhyme with a, call it b. Any end word that rhymes with b is also called b. Keep moving through the alphabet giving code letters to further end words. Give the same letter to all words that rhyme.

I hope that doesn't sound too complicated. These are the end words of my verse and the way they rhyme : doing – a / mad – b / answered – c / sad – b.

The way a verse or poem rhymes is called its *rhyme scheme*. There are all sorts of different ones. Some common examples are a b b a, b a a b, c d d c, d c c d and so on.

The only other thing I want to say about rhyme just now is to mention the *rhyming couplet* (meaning 'couple', two). These are two lines with end rhymes that usually finish off a poem. As an example, William Shakespeare's sonnet number 18, 'Shall I compare thee to a summer's day?', ends like this:

So long as men can breathe or eyes can see,
So long lives this, and this gives life to thee.

A rhyming couplet is sometimes just the right way to round off a poem.

However, back to the topic of this module, which is 'uni-verses' – simple one-verse poems that give you a chance to practise rhythm and rhyme schemes. Here's a verse I've written:

What do you put into Halloween pie?
A bat's leather wing, a chameleon's eye,
A crystal of frost and a red lick of fire,
Midnight's deep hush – then a scream rising higher . . .

Here's its rhythm:

    / ^ ^ / ^ ^ / ^ ^ /
da-duh-duh *da*-duh-duh *da*-duh-duh *da*

And the rhyme scheme is a a b b c c etc. The poem is called 'Halloween Pie' (www.routledge.com/professional/9780415477529).

One way of becoming more familiar with rhythm and rhyme is to copy patterns that already exist. Instead of Halloween pie, you could cook up a Christmas Day pie, or a holiday pie, or a Bonfire Night pie or – well, you get the idea.

FOR THE PUPIL

'Myku'

Teacher's note: You may wish to read the notes on **Haiku** (**Module 7**), before working with the pupils on myku poems.)

What is a myku?

If you thought that 'uni-verse' was a bad pun, then 'myku' is even worse! There's a kind of little poem that comes from Japan called a *haiku*. You'll read more about those in **Haiku** (**Module 7**). I like haiku very much and enjoy working with pupils to help them write their own. Some kids were finding it hard to get the hang of haiku, so I invented my own version – my haiku – myku – get it?

A myku poem is really simple. It has only three lines. The first line has two syllables, the second line three syllables, and the third line four syllables. Here's one of my myku (I thought I was starting to stammer then):

Old goat
Dazed on years –
A summer moon.

That's all there is to it. The story behind this poem is that at the back of our house on a patch of grass there's this old goat called Gordon. He's very ancient and looking really thin, though he still eats like a – well, goat, I suppose. Last summer there was a beautiful fat full moon one evening, and Gordon was standing out under the warm sky. And for once he was not nibbling grass but seemed to be staring up at the heavens. It would have made a great picture, but I didn't have a camera. So I wrote that myku instead. It's like a little snapshot picture of that moment, which is what myku poems tend to be like. And when Gordon has gone I'll have that poem like a keepsake to remember him forever.

Here are a couple more.

Spring dawn.
Kiss goodbye –
Who knows what now?

Module 13

About a year ago I had to catch an early train. I was on the platform, and there was a young couple near by. The boy was seeing his girlfriend off and as the train pulled in he gave her a kiss. He looked quite upset and I wondered what was going on – although I could hardly go up to him and ask! So I wrote the myku instead.

The point is that, when I read it again just now to put in this book, the whole scene came back to me very clearly. *I might have completely forgotten about it otherwise.* Writing myku is a great way of jogging your memory (remember Donna?) and takes a lot less time than keeping a diary.

Another important point is that, if I hadn't told you the story about that couple, you wouldn't know about them by reading the myku. That's fine. Instead you would have had your own thoughts and maybe memories and feelings. The poem might have meant something very different to you. And that's another value of poetry – it can mean different things to different people, and there's no need to feel anxious that your ideas are wrong and another person's are right. OK, one more from me:

Sunday
Churchbells ring –
Who calls to whom?

I think quite a lot about God and life and What Does It All Mean. I heard these churchbells ringing, and they sounded so joyous, and the people walking up to the church looked very happy. It got me thinking, and the myku I wrote simply asks a question that came to my mind. I don't have an answer to it yet.

Take a look at the myku on page 101 (Figure 8). They were written by Year 5 pupils in a workshop. I showed the group a picture of a windy street corner. There's a frightened cat crouching in the shadows, and in the background what looks like a firework is exploding in the sky. We talked about the picture for a while and then the kids got busy . . .

I think these are pretty good. The pupils enjoyed writing them too, partly because they didn't take long. Also you get that great feeling of having finished something. Although everyone agreed that choosing the words carefully was very important.

Writing your own myku

If you'd like to try writing myku of your own, notice something around you and away you go. Or you could look back at 'Hare and Cosmos' on page 12 and use that for your inspiration.

Howling wind
Whipping my face,
alone.

Cold night,
Blowing wind.
Get home safely

Ghost town
scared to death
deadly pathway.

Haunted
shivering.
a lightning flash.

Ghost town,
icy breeze,
always raining.

I saw
leaves falling
on the wet road.

The trees
crashing and
hushing all night.

Bare trees
scattered leaves –
Autumn has come.

Darkness.
A shadow.
I stand alone.

(Fireworks)
High, sharp,
straight up-round –
silver, blue, red!

Figure 8

The next batch of modules explores some slightly more extended forms of poetry. So why not look at the flowchart and take your shovel – I mean, take your pick.

List poems

(There are no teacher's notes for this module.)

One value of list poems is that they make you look around and notice things. When you've gathered up some ideas you create your list. This is a very free-and-easy form of poem: there are no rules. You can slip in a little rhythm, invent some rhymes, play around with the words on the page – or do none of those things. Here's one I did about the kind of Christmas stocking I used to get as a boy (I get socks and hankies now and that's not as much fun):

Christmas Stocking –
crackly paper
oranges and apples sweet and tangy
chocolate money
plastic made-in-HongKong rockets
sheriff's badge
pair of socks (from Auntie May, handknitted)
a colouring book
and pencils that smell of Friday afternoons in school
a bag of dinosaurs, red, blue, brown and green
a false nose
a set of magic tricks
a crepe paper cracker with glossy band
a rattly handful of walnuts at the bottom
a thread of cotton
a few sparks of glitter . . .

I wish I could live inside here
forever!

Another list poem ('My Place') with more structure to it can be found at www.routledge.com/professional/9780415477529. You can experiment with the idea of list poems in various ways. The one on the facing page uses the notion of 'if – then', which forms the basis of each line. Lists like this can be funny or serious. Guess which is which on the facing page . . .

Module 12

If pigs could fly then the price of bacon would rise.
If horses could fly we'd have to take shelter!
(And Pegasus-steeds in their millions would whirl in flocks across
     the skies.)
If elephants could fly nobody would venture outside.
If poets could fly they'd have their heads in the clouds (maybe they
     already do).
If teachers could fly we'd get higher marks.

If wishes were stones there'd be mountains by now.
If curses were sand there'd be a desert by now.
If anger were raindrops there'd be an ocean by now.
If forgiveness were jewels the world would be poor by now.

If you like the idea of lists poems then you might also enjoy the challenge of
Counting poems (Module 11).

Counting poems

(There are no teacher's notes for this module.)

This is one step on from simple list poems. Again it's a free-and-easy form that you can play with in all kinds of ways. Here are a few ideas:

▶ Character descriptions. Think about yourself or a fictional character and create a description counting up from one (you can miss out numbers if you want).

> Steve B –
> One heart
> Two ears
> Three eyes (including one poetical)
> Four shoes (best pair, scruffy pair)
> Five pages written so far today
> Six books at the bedside waiting to be read
> Seven is a favourite number
> Eight shirts (three in the wash)
> Nine story ideas buzzing in his brain
> Ten fingers (including two thumbs) clattering around the keyboard.

Activity: Counting with dice

The same kind of 'free-flow verse' is very flexible and works for all kinds of topics, such as classrooms or schools generally, parties and gatherings, the High Street, a favourite book – you name it, you can count it.

▶ Look back at the word grid, Table 2 on page 22. Choosing items for yourself or else randomly using a dice, count up from one to ten like this:

> 1   proud castle on the hill.
> 2   tall trees that grow beside a mill.
> 3   brown crispy leaves blowing in the wind.
> 4   backwards walking men going on a binge.
> 5   nasty growling dogs searching for a feast.
> 6   white tipped mountains facing to the East.

7　flying fairies trying out their wings.

8　precious diamonds belonging to the King.

9　brilliant shooting stars hurtling through the sky.

10　devil hunters that give the evil eye.

This was written by a group of ten-year-olds. I gave the first line to help establish a rhythm and we all worked together on the rhyme.

Or you can simply pick a topic and build on it using the same kind of structure – check out 'One Red Robin' at www.routledge.com/professional/9780415477529.

Counting poems are good fun to read aloud in a group. Have a look at the next module for more ideas about this.

Chorus poems and chants

Resources

Great resources for traditional British chants, riddle rhymes and playground verses are J. O. Halliwell's *Popular Rhymes & Nursery Tales of England* and Iona and Peter Opie's *I Saw Esau*. Also, an Internet search yields a wealth of material. Two good sites I found are www.beachnet.com/~jeanettem/chants.html#SAY, which is a treasure trove of chants, taunts, clapping games and skipping-rope rhymes from the US, and www.zelo.com/family/nursery/oneforsorrow.asp, which gives a wide selection of rhymes.

Chorus poems and chants

I'm writing about this sort of poem mainly because I've noticed that when groups make a poem in class they often like to read it out together. There's nothing stopping you from doing this with any kind of poetry really, although obviously poems with rhythm and rhyme work best.

The next step up from just reading in unison is to create poems especially for two or more voices. For the sake of convenience, we'll say that a chorus poem is one where certain parts are intended for many voices to speak together, while chants use a lot of repetition intended for more than one voice.

The history of the chorus and the chant

The idea of a chorus goes back to Ancient Greek drama, and its job was often to tell the audience things that the main characters couldn't say, such as their thoughts and feelings. Because what the chorus said had to be made very clear, they also used other techniques such as moving together, echo effects and masks that showed exaggerated facial expressions.

A chant is a rhythmic speaking or singing of words and sounds and, like the chorus, goes back a long way in history. The word itself comes from the Greek and means *a ringing sound*. Chanting is a vital part of some religious practices, but we hear chants often in everyday life – for instance the chanting of crowds at sports matches, in rock songs (Queen's 'We Will Rock You' is a great example) and in rap music, where words are often spoken rather than sung. Chanting has also been an important part of traditional playground games. Here's one from America:

> Cinderella, dressed in yella,
> Went upstairs to kiss a fella,
> Made a mistake, kissed a snake,
> How many doctors will it take?
> 2–4–6–8 etc.

And from Britain:

Magpies

One for sorrow,
Two for joy,
Three for a girl,
Four for a boy,
Five for silver,
Six for gold,
Seven for a secret
Never to be told.

Another variation of this is:

One for anger,
Two for mirth,
Three for a wedding,
Four for a birth,
Five for rich and
Six for poor,
Seven for a witch –
I can tell you no more!

And from Africa:

Vusi drives the kombi that takes us all to school.
We open all the windows so the air blows nice and cool.
He hoots when he fetches us, he hoots when he goes,
He hoots at the cows that are standing in the road.
Vusi drives the kombi that we all love to ride.
If you want to travel with us, there's lots of room inside!

(A kombi is a small passenger van, and Vusi is a common Zulu name.)

You can see that counting poems are very like the chants and chorus poems above. One good way of creating a chant is to use the rhythm and rhyme scheme of one that already exists. Simply think of a new topic and the words are likely to come into your mind very easily. Use the poems above for instance, or fit new words to my 'Halloween Pie'. If you want a structure for a non-rhyming chant, look at 'Vampire Chant' (www.routledge.com/professional/9780415477529).

'Adding' poems

These are also called cumulative poems. The idea is to think of a theme and provide the first two or four lines, then pass the poem on to another pupil or group to add a couplet. Then *they* pass it on until it's been round the class. The example below copies the rhyme and metre of a well-known poem by W. H. Hudson (1871–1940) called 'Leisure':

> What is this life if, full of care,
> We never hug a teddy bear?
> Or blow some bubbles, pillow fight,
> Or stand and watch the sunset light?

(And always end as you started –)

> A poor life this if, full of care,
> We never hug a teddy bear.

The next couple of modules look at poems that are funny and puzzling – limericks and riddles. So if you want to chuckle and then scratch your head, go and investigate.

Limericks

> The limerick packs laughs anatomical
> Into space that is quite economical,
> But the good ones I've seen
> So seldom are clean,
> And the clean ones so seldom are comical.

The history of limericks

This anonymous verse highlights the fact that traditional limericks were usually subversive and often obscene. Their origins are obscure, though they were popularised in the last century by Edward Lear (1812–1888), who is also well known more generally for his nonsense verse.

Resources

Although limericks can be highly sophisticated insofar as they say a lot in few words, using subtle variations of rhythm and clever rhymes, a simpler, stricter structure is more suitable for younger and more innocent (?) writers. A useful web page containing some pretty good examples is www.teachingideas.co.uk/ English/limerick.htm. The best way of helping pupils to create their own limericks is to read plenty to the class and have a go at writing some yourself.

Limericks

I once knew a young man called Ray
Whose head was stuck on the wrong way
And while never knowing
Just where he was going
He knew where he'd been straight away.

That's a limerick. As you can see it has five lines, a definite rhythm and a rhyme scheme that goes <u>a a b b a</u>. You'll also notice that lines three and four are a bit shorter than the others. Limericks are usually funny (or try to be) and were originally very naughty. If you ask your teacher to tell you some rude limericks – you will almost certainly get into trouble. Here's another one –

I knew a young lady called Jean
Who ate nothing but stew and baked beans
I squeezed her once nightly
A little too tightly –
She exploded into smithereens.

As you can see a limerick can tell a little story or describe an incident. Often the first line ends with the name of the person the story is about, or the place where it happens . . .

I once knew a girl from Skegness
Whose hair was a big scruffy mess.
I told her to brush it
And added 'Don't rush it,
And change that bin-bag for a dress.'

Making a limerick

When I want to write a limerick I usually make up the first line to begin with and see where it takes me. I think of a name (person or place) that has lots of rhymes. Here are a few starters if you'd like to have a go:

I once knew a young man called Peter
Who drove a fast snazzy two-seater . . .

I once met a man from Dundee
Whose two legs were locked at the knee . . .

I met a young woman from Brent
Who smelt of a strange kind of scent . . .

And here are a few last lines so you can try working backwards:

▶ And now he's a footballing star.

▶ She escaped in a hot air balloon.

▶ They just wandered around for a while.

▶ 'And don't ever do it again!'

▶ And that was the end of our school.

Now what am I talking about below?

Whoever makes it tells it not,
Whoever takes it knows it not,
Whoever knows it wants it not.

To find out you have to go to the next module – **Riddles** (**Module 8**).

FOR THE PUPIL

Riddles

(There are no teacher's notes for this module.)

The answer is counterfeit (false) money. A riddle – as you've worked out – is a puzzle. The word itself goes back to Old English, meaning 'opinion' or 'to interpret' (have your own ideas about), and even further back to an Ancient Greek word meaning 'to fit'. So a riddle is a word puzzle where you have to fit your meaning around the clues. You'll see that riddles can include an important feature of some poems – repetition. I said, repetition. I wonder if you can create a three-line riddle using the same pattern. Here's one I tried.

> Whoever makes it masters it not.
> Whoever ignores it understands it not.
> Whoever respects it suffers by it not.

The answer to my riddle is *fire*.

Puzzling stuff!

Sometimes riddles are written in rhyme. This one has three kinds of puzzle tangled up in it.

> My first is in rock but never in stone,
> My second's in marrow but not in the bone.
> My third's in the bolster but not in the bed
> And my fourth's not in living and neither in dead.

The first puzzle is just *what is* 'the first', 'the second' etc. Well the answer is a letter. My first letter is in the word 'rock' but not in the word 'stone', and so on. So the second puzzle in this riddle is to find the letters that make up the solution. But there's a sting in the tail, because the letter we're looking for is neither in the word living nor in dead. That's the third twist in the puzzle. If I was really cruel I could just let you sweat over the answer – but I won't because I'm kind. The solution is the letter 'r'. Once you know the secret you'll see that this kind of riddle is not difficult to make up. Take another letter of the alphabet and see if you can copy the structure of the verse above. I tried and came up with this:

Module
8

My first is in silent but never in loud.
My second's in single but not in the crowd.
My third is in whisper and also in shout.
My fourth is in 'Shut up!' – so what's it about?

The answer is the letter 's'. Notice that the rhyme scheme is <u>a a b b</u>. If you feel like experimenting you can play with other patterns, <u>a b b a</u> or <u>a b a b</u> for example – or others if you extend the verse beyond four lines.

Metaphors as riddles

Another feature of riddles is that they are often metaphors. In other words what the riddle describes is a comparison with something else. Here's an example:

Thirty-two white horses on the red hills.
Now they stamp, now they champ,
Now they stand still.

The number thirty-two is a big clue, for we have thirty-two teeth in our mouths (if we've got a full set). So teeth are being compared to white horses, while the red hills refer to our gums. Can you think of a metaphor riddle like this? It needn't have rhyme or rhythm, but it can if you want it to. Here's one I did:

A gleaming white pearl afloat in the night
Looking surprised as it sinks out of sight.

You'll probably find that easy. The answer is the full moon. When I look at the 'face' in the full moon it always looks startled to me. If it doesn't to you then I guess my riddle won't make much sense!

Many riddles these days are posed as simple questions. For example:

1   What goes up the stairs and down without moving?
2   What can you catch but not throw?
3   The more of me there is, the less you see. What am I?
4   What can fill a room but takes up no space?

And the answers are: 1: stair carpet; 2: a cold; 3: fog or mist; and 4: noise or light. This web page has lots of similar riddles: www.teacherneedhelp.com/students/riddles.htm.

Search out some further examples and see if you can turn some into the kinds of riddle rhymes we've looked at in this module. If you really get into riddling you might end up writing longer poems that pose a puzzle. I did one that you'll find at www.routledge.com/professional/9780415477529. I gave it the brilliantly original title 'A Riddle'.

Take it further

At this point you have a choice. If you want to explore the fascinating Japanese forms of poetry called *haiku*, leap to the next module. If you want to find out about more extended forms of poetry, check out the flowchart and go to the next batch of modules. If you'd prefer to go home and watch TV and play computer games, just ask your teacher and I'm sure that will be fine.

Haiku

Writing a haiku

Writing haiku poems is a common activity in many schools, and the three-line 5–7–5 syllable structure is familiar to the majority of pupils. It may be that haiku are popular (though I mustn't be cynical about this) because they are quick and easy. Virtually any pupil can throw together such a poem, which actually sounds pretty good . . .

> The wind howled all night,
> Clouds streamed across the wide sky.
> Trees stood lonely, lost.

That example is in fact adapted from a guidebook on poetry writing for adults, and both poem and commentary completely fail to grasp the elegance and power that the haiku form can embody and the challenge it presents in the composition. The author of the book tells us that a haiku* such as the one above establishes an 'atmosphere' and may be a jumping-off point for a more extended poem that could, in the end, abandon the haiku form altogether, its purpose having been served. That's a bit like suggesting the use of a fine crystal goblet for drinking cola.

Not that I should be too precious about this, because for many years I churned out scores of haiku and felt justly proud of myself before I read a word about the subtle and complex nuances of the form, its venerable history and the often deeply spiritual nature of its aim.

So does that mean my argument is self-defeating; that I've elevated haiku to the point where pupils shouldn't try to write them because their efforts will invariably fall short? Not at all. My opinion is that to attempt haiku just because they seem easy is pointless, whereas to write with even a little awareness of the subtlety and strength of the form is an effort to be celebrated.

★ 'Haiku' is used as both singular and plural.

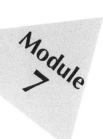

Module 7

Useful classroom tips

At the very least I think that pupils should appreciate these ideas about haiku:

▶ Traditionally, haiku poetry often presents an observation of a natural and commonplace event.

▶ The language is plain, simple and direct without 'verbal trickery' (as the poet and translator Lucien Stryk puts it).

▶ The observation of the ordinary may suggest its connection to 'the greater whole', and usually indicates the spiritual heart of the poem.

▶ The traditional structure of the haiku is made up of two elements: the setting of the scene or situation, followed by a sudden perception resulting from it. The two elements are usually divided by a break, which in English translations is often a dash – indicating a sudden change (or in our case a sudden development) of thought.

Haiku

Haiku is a form of poetry that came from ancient Japan. This is a haiku poem:

> Burned out car. Wasteland –
> Willowherb blooms anyway,
> October morning.

What do you notice about it? Chat with your friends if you like and write down your ideas before reading on . . .

It has three lines. It is in the present tense. The syllables in the lines are 5–7–5. It doesn't rhyme. There is a dash (–) at the end of the first line. It mentions a particular time of the year and day. It shows a contrast between something dead and ruined (the car and the wasteland) and something alive and growing (the willowherb, which is a tall weed with pinky-purple flowers). It is intended to help you realise that, even out of something ruined, life can appear. In other words, there's a big idea wrapped up in a little poem.

Many haiku poems are something like this. Maybe you've written them before, following that pattern of 5–7–5 syllables. If you have, that's good practice for what I'll ask you to do now.

That dash in the poem is important. It separates something ordinary that the poet *notices* from something important that he *realises*. In other words, out of noticing something small and ordinary grew a big idea. So the basic plan of these haiku poems is:

> Look I've noticed this –
> Wow! I've realised *this*.

Here's another:

> Grey factory smoke
> My eyes follow upwards – Look!
> Starlings still gather.

The theme of this haiku is the same as the first, that 'life will find a way'. I had the idea for both of these poems when I found myself in the industrial area of town. That's one of the great things about haiku, that you can have ideas for them by being just where you are and using your eyes in this special way.

Having said that haiku follow a plan, you don't need to be too strict about it.

> Like tumbling leaves
> Thoughts, worries, soon blow away
> In little cat's mind.

You see that I haven't obeyed all of the 'rules' of haiku poetry every time, and that's just fine. Some very famous haiku poets deliberately broke the rules because they stopped the writers from saying what they wanted to say. So if you decide to make some haiku, have a go at keeping to the rules, but don't let them restrict you.

There's more about haiku on our website at www.routledge.com/professional/ 9780415477529. Or, if you prefer, the next batch of modules looks at slightly longer and more complex kinds of poetry. Why don't you dive over there now and take a look? Go on, I dare you.

Worsery rhymes

(There are no teacher's notes for this module.)

Copycat!

The next couple of modules are all about copying. Now I know this is usually frowned on in school, and in most cases that's quite right. But in the world of writing (and other kinds of artistry as well), a good way of learning how to do something is by following in someone else's footsteps. By copying the verse forms that someone else has used you'll become more familiar with those forms yourself. By copying the style, theme and tone of other poets you'll find a style, themes and moods that suit you and express what *you* want to say. By following the rules and getting to know them you'll be able to use them more flexibly for yourself.

Apart from all of that, copying what other poets have done is part of the 'learning through play' attitude that I think helps us to improve as writers.

Writing a worsery rhyme

A friend of mine gets great enjoyment writing what he calls 'worsery rhymes'. These are based on nursery rhymes and traditional chants and sayings, but with a twist. So, for instance . . .

Jack and Jill went up the hill
To have a kiss and cuddle. It never happened, sad to say,
For Jack fell in a puddle.

Here's another that we all know:

I scream, you scream
We all scream for ice-cream.

And here are a few from pupils in a school I visited:

I holler, you holler
We all holler for Coca Cola®

I skip, you skip
We all skip and then slip.

I run, you run
We all run for sticky buns.

Repartee rhymes

This next example is called a 'repartee rhyme'. Repartee is a clever, quick-fire reply to a question.

> Have you got a sister?
> *The postman just kissed her.*
>
> Have you got an uncle?
> *On his head a big carbuncle.*
>
> Have you got a cat?
> *The lorry squashed him flat.*
>
> Have you got a teacher?
> *On the phone I try to reach her.*
>
> Have you got some hair?
> *In my armpits – just look there!*

Activity: A bag full of questions

As you see, repartee rhymes can be silly and cheeky. A good game is to work with your friends and write lots of questions and put them in a bag. Get someone to pull them out one at a time and see what answers pop into mind. You'll create a group poem very quickly this way.

Here's a short character poem:

> Charlie Charlie in the tub
> Charlie Charlie pulled the plug –
> Oh my goodness, oh my soul
> There goes Charlie down the hole!

What other adventures can you make up for Charlie? How about –

> Charlie Charlie in the car
> Charlie Charlie went too far –
> Oh my goodness, oh my life
> Now he's got an ugly wife!

This is a skipping-rope rhyme. The regular rhythm helped to keep the skipping rope to time.

> Spanish lady turn around
> Spanish lady touch the ground
> Spanish lady do high kicks
> Spanish lady do the splits.

I'm sure you can think of lots of other versions . . .

> Rubber baby bouncing high
> Rubber baby to the sky
> Rubber baby make me smile
> Rubber baby bounce a mile.

Here's a traditional counting rhyme that you surely know:

> One, two, buckle my shoe
> Three, four, knock at the door
> Five, six, pick up sticks
> Seven, eight, lay them straight
> Nine, ten, a big fat hen
> Eleven, twelve, dig and delve
> Thirteen, fourteen, maids a-courting
> Fifteen, sixteen, maids in the kitchen
> Seventeen, eighteen, maids in waiting
> Nineteen, twenty, my plate's empty

Here's how I changed it:

> One two visiting you
> Three four knock at the door
> Five six playing your tricks
> Seven eight saying I'm late
> Nine ten knocking again
> Eleven twelve admiring yourself
> Thirteen fourteen you've gone a-courting
> Fifteen sixteen bell needs fixing
> Seventeen eighteen I'm still waiting
> Nineteen twenty – house is empty!

You can find plenty of rhymes to change on the Internet. A good website is www.rhymes.org.uk/.

If you want to learn more about copying the style and structure of poems, click over to our website at www.routledge.com/professional/9780415477529. Or you can blast into orbit and head straight for **Genre poems (Module 5)!**

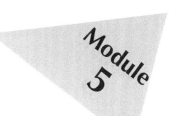

Module 5

Genre poems

Exploring interests

When I work with pupils I encourage them to make poems about their own interests and hobbies. They are usually very motivated to do this, while reading out their work is an opportunity to 'legitimately' share their passion. I remember that one boy was a little embarrassed to read out because all he loved doing, so he told me, was playing video games. I pointed out that plenty of grown-up poets did that too and mentioned a collection called *Techno Talk* where he could read other poems about video games and computers. On another occasion I was able to exploit a boy's interest in fishing and introduced him to Ted Hughes's poem 'Pike'. He subsequently used it as a template for a poem of his own. Pupils' ongoing interest in Harry Potter and other fantasy worlds can be used as a springboard into fantastical and magical poems. One excellent collection is *The Puffin Book of Magic Verse*, which is currently out of print, although used copies are readily available through, for instance, Amazon.co.uk.

Creating a mental framework

Finally, research in the neurosciences increasingly confirms what has been known for millennia – that rhythmical poems, songs and chants aid memory. Ancient bardic storytellers knew nothing of the reticular activating system, yet still understood that metre and rhyme create a mental framework within which huge quantities of information can be held ready to be made available at will.

I suggest that an enjoyable and robust way of helping pupils to understand and remember factual material is to get them to write verses about it. My friend Tim Harding's work will show you the way (www.routledge.com/professional/ 9780415477529).

Genre poems

You have probably come across the word *genre* in Literacy and English lessons. Fantasy is one genre; horror, romance, animal adventure and science fiction (SF) are others. The word genre means 'kind' or 'style' (and perhaps you won't be surprised to learn that it's linked with the word 'gender').

No doubt you've written genre stories – but have you ever thought of trying your hand at genre poems? Most fans of any genre usually know a lot about it. For instance, although I like *Doctor Who* (and remember watching the very first episode when I was a boy), kids who watch the programme today know much more about it than I do (and have better sets of trading cards!). A *Doctor Who* fan would have plenty of knowledge to think up many ideas for a poem, which could be fitted into just about any of the forms of poetry we've looked at.

Here are two SF haiku poems. I call them 'high-ku' (another bad pun, sorry).

> An old sad spaceman
> can only look up and sigh,
> his last flight over.
>
> Long years of searching
> are done. We're home now with this
> alien flower.

And a couple of horror ones:

> Drinking the moonlight,
> all the world's red rage I howl –
> dark lonely misfit.
>
> From this high tower
> see my vampire smile, because
> the world's gone crazy.

Why use a genre?

Another value of genre poems is that they help to bring ideas alive. By that I mean you might read some facts about, say, the planet Mars and marvel at the incredible

FOR THE PUPIL

pictures beamed back from there by space probes. But when you write a poem about it you *go there* in your imagination, which can be a very powerful experience. That happened to me when I wrote 'Tharsis', which you'll find at www.routledge.com/professional/9780415477529. Tharsis, by the way, is a huge volcanic plateau near the equator of Mars.

If you read the poem you'll see that it neither rhymes nor has a regular rhythm. That kind of poetry is called *free verse*, and we'll be looking at it more closely in **Module 3**.

The main point of this module is to suggest that what you are interested in can inspire you. There are more notes about that on our website. Also you can learn there about how genre poems can help you learn and remember facts (www.routledge.com/professional/9780415477529).

Take it further

The next few modules deal with free verse (which doesn't have rhythm or rhyme); blank verse (which has rhythm but no rhyme); and a few unusual verse forms you might like to play with. Look at the flowchart and take your pick.

Blank verse/ free verse

Blank verse

Blank verse is unrhymed iambic pentameter – in other words each line contains five iambs (^/) as in:

```
^  /   ^   /  ^   /  ^  /    ^   /
```
I wake and feel the fell of dark, not day.

If handled well, the use of blank verse evokes the lambent rise and fall of the voice, without the sense of a rigid structure being imposed upon the lines. This is especially true when the writer varies the pattern a little: unremitting iambic pentameter, unrhymed or not, can sound clumpy and monotonous. The deliberate avoidance of rhyme – or the inclusion of half rhymes and other subtle echoes – adds to the listener's pleasure.

Because blank verse is a common and popular form – indeed it is the main form used in dramatic poetry in English – I think that pupils should at least be aware of its existence. When they become more attuned to, and familiar with, the lilt of blank verse, they will have another tool in their craftbox when it comes to writing poetry of their own.

Useful classroom tips

One quick and effective way of achieving this is to help pupils create lines made up of iambic pentameter and deliberately to overemphasise the rhythm. Twenty minutes of this 'locks' some pupils into the form, and they delight in trying to speak like it for the rest of the lesson. Initially get them to clap out the rhythm in lines such as:

▶ Please give us extra homework straight away.

▶ I'll share my sweets with teachers and my friends.

▶ I will behave and never mess about.

Then encourage the pupils to create similar lines of their own (although they might choose different topics). Once the pattern of the blank verse line has been embedded, read something perhaps from Shakespeare (who used the form extensively), but 'easing off' so that the rhythm is more subtle and serves more as 'background music' to the words themselves and their meaning:

> But soft! What light through yonder
>   window breaks?
> It is the East, and Juliet is the sun.
> Arise, fair sun, and kill the envious moon,
> Who is already sick and pale with grief
> That thou her maid art more fair than
>   she.
> Be not her maid, since she is envious;
> Her vestal livery is but sick and green,
> And none but fools do wear it; cast it off.
> It is my lady: O, it is my love!

Free verse

Free verse on the other hand neither rhymes nor has a regular rhythm, but uses what editor and reviewer Roger Elkin calls 'cadential rhythm', the rise and fall of the human voice, to create the 'breathing pulse' of the poem. An important aspect of the art of writing free verse is to be sensitive to the way in which the voice and the fluidity of breathing work together to enhance the meaning of the words. This will be reflected in the poet's decisions about where line breaks should occur, thus guiding the reader towards the pace and emphasis that the poet intends. Looking again at the poem 'Tharsis', for example, we see that the lines are short and line breaks are frequent. The eye is led swiftly down the page, and this creates the tendency to read the words more quickly. The hurrying voice echoes the mad rush of the Martian wind, while the visual appearance of the poem is 'jagged' and almost chaotic, suggesting the landscape it describes.

Many more examples of free verse (used much more elegantly than I can achieve) are easily to be found. Contrast, for instance, Ted Hughes's poem 'The Express', previously mentioned on page 40, with his poem 'The Horses' (from *Selected Poems 1957–1967*). Presume that every line break, the positioning of every word and the placing of every piece of punctuation are deliberate. How do all of these things draw out the sense of the language and enhance its descriptive power? When you read the poems aloud do you find that you are guided towards reading them in a

certain way – that your voice is almost urged forwards, spurred on or held back by the way the words are set out on the page?

The very existence of free verse has provoked some strong reactions in the world of poetry. My own feeling is that it does have value as a legitimate form, at the very least for the reasons outlined above. It is not an easy option when writing poetry, and when pupils are exposed to its subtleties their appreciation of the interplay between sound and sense in language is likely to benefit.

Useful classroom tip

In introducing pupils to free verse you might remind them of the work they did on shape poems. Here too the emphasis is on the visual arrangement of phrases and sentences to reflect what the poem is about.

Blank verse

Read these lines out loud:

1   I'm having bacon and eggs for my tea.

2   I'm having eggs and bacon for my tea.

3   There's only one egg left upon my plate.

4   No doubt my brother David pinched the rest.

5   I'll wallop him when he comes back from the shops.

6   I'll bash him when he comes back from the shops.

7   'Mind you,' said Mum, 'he is a growing boy.'

8   'Mind you, he is a growing boy,' said Mum.

Did you notice that most of them had a kind of 'bouncy' quality when you spoke them? A couple didn't have that bounce – numbers 1 and 5 (although if you say the word 'wallop' really quickly it will fit the rhythm). And it's rhythm that we're talking about again; a particular kind of rhythm – let's make it very clear. Say the word 'today' five times – today, today, today, today, today. When you said it, did you find yourself putting more 'weight' on the syllable 'day'? Say it again five times and clap it out as well. As I write it below I'll put this mark / where you clap and this mark ^ where you don't clap.

     ^ /   ^ /   ^ /   ^ /   ^ /
    Today, today, today, today, today.

That pattern works for the bouncy lines at the top of the module. Mark them out in the same way that I've done. Now take away numbers one and five. This is what we've got:

> I'm having eggs and bacon for my tea.
> There's only one egg left upon my plate.
> No doubt my brother David pinched the rest.
> I'll bash him when he comes back from the shops.
> 'Mind you,' said Mum, 'he is a growing boy.'

I took out number eight as well because that's almost the same as number seven. We now have a sequence of rhythmical lines, but they don't rhyme. Notice too that each line is a complete sentence, though it doesn't have to be. We can run any sentence beyond one line, but let's try and keep the rhythm going.

> I'm having eggs and bacon for my tea
> although they say it's bad to have too much.
> Oh no! There's only one egg on my plate,
> because I think my brother pinched the rest.
> I'll bash him when he comes back from the shops.
> 'Mind you,' said Mum, 'he is a growing boy.'

Blank verse

This kind of poetry is called *blank verse*. You can tell when it's being used because the lines have the rhythm we've just looked at but don't have any obvious rhyme. People who write blank verse poems do vary the rhythm because it can sound a bit tedious – if you always write the words the same, with never any diff'rences between, the same old rhythm each and every time. I'm sure you understand what I've just said.

Anyway, if you fancy playing with blank verse, just imagine a little scene like the one above and write down what happened using the rhythm you've learned.

FOR THE PUPIL

Free verse

Another kind of verse is called *free verse*, because it has neither rhyme nor rhythm. But it's not the same as the kind of language you find in storybooks, just line upon line of writing. In free verse the lines are broken deliberately at certain points and continued on the line below. We touched on this idea when we looked at the poem 'Donna Didn't Come Back' (www.routledge.com/professional/9780415477529). That's a free verse poem, and it's a *poem* rather than ordinary writing (or prose), partly because of the way that the words are laid out on the page. I could, of course, have arranged the words differently, but I set them out like that on purpose. Look at the poem again and think about why I made those decisions.

My science fiction poem 'Tharsis' is also written in free verse (www.routledge.com/professional/9780415477529). Speak with your teacher about why I decided to set it out as I did.

Writing poetry can be tricky!

It's important for you to realise that, while it might be hard work to make poems rhyme and have rhythm, writing free verse is not the easy way out. You have to think just as much and make as many decisions as you plan how to break the lines and set out the words on the page. If you've already written poems that don't have rhythm or rhyme, have another look at them now to see if you would choose to set them out differently.

We're going to spend our last-but-one module before BLASTOFF! looking at some unusual forms of poetry. Perhaps you'll consider choosing one and have a go at making a poem of your own?

Module 2

Some other forms

(**Teacher's note:** There are scores of different verse forms. The ones here are just a handful that appeal to me. A useful website for finding even more is www.shadowpoetry.com/resources/wip/types.html.)

You know that in sport you have to play by the rules. They are there to make the game more enjoyable for both the players and the spectators. Also, if the rules are applied fairly and well they can bring out the players' best performance. The rules in that case are there to support and guide, not to limit and trap those who follow them. In fact, the word 'rule' comes from the Latin word 'to lead straight and direct', and further back from the Greek 'to stretch out'. Perhaps that means stretching your imagination and skill?

The rules of language

We have plenty of rules in the way we use language too – not just when we write but also when we speak. Maybe as you talk to friends you don't realise that you are following all kinds of rules and so are they, otherwise you wouldn't be able to understand each other! The rhyme, rhythm and other elements of poetry that we've been looking at in this book are there to lead you 'straight and direct' to what you'd like to say; to the ideas and feelings you want to express. They are not there to trap you or limit you.

Bending the rules

However, I think that things are easier when writing poetry than when playing sport, because in poetry you can bend the rules creatively without getting into trouble. Below are several different kinds of poems that perhaps you haven't heard about before. I've picked them because I think they are fun and offer a creative challenge. All of these forms were invented by somebody, some of them quite recently. And you never know, maybe if you work on your poetry writing then one day you might invent a new form too. Look through these and pick a couple to play with.

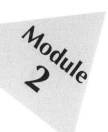

Acrostic poem

An acrostic is where the first letter of each line spells a word, which is usually the subject of the description. For example 'wordsmith' could be turned into an acrostic poem:

> Wonderment in seeing
> Ordinary people, places, moments of my life
> Rolled around the mind,
> Dropped carefully on the page,
> Stitched in my memory;
> Musically chimed and patterned;
> Interwoven meanings
> Threaded on the
> Heart of my life.

That's my way of making 'wordsmith' into a poem. You could use the same word and make a completely different poem, or choose some other word as an acrostic.

Brevette

That word means 'brief' or short, and in fact this is a poem of only three words! But they have to be written in this order – subject (noun), verb, object (noun). The verb usually ends in s. That's about it really, and this is what it looks like:

> Mouse
> nibbles
> cheese.

> Poet
> embroiders
> meanings.

If you want to bend the rules try noun – verb – adverb (and can you use alliteration as well?):

> Balloons
> bump
> boisterously.

> Dinosaurs
> dance
> delicately.

Brevettes
bubble
briefly.

Clerihew

This is a comic four-line poem that uses the rhyme scheme a a b b (i.e. it's made of two rhyming couplets). The form was invented by Edmund Clerihew Bentley (1875–1956). The first line usually names a person, and the second line usually tells us something about them, which is then developed through the third and fourth lines.

Mr Oliver Stand
Played drums in the band,
But couldn't follow the beat
With his hands or his feet.

Miss Julia Style
Ran the four-minute mile
With no one to beat her.
This poem has metre!

Essence

This kind of poem looks simple but needs careful thought. There are only two lines, but each has six syllables and there must be an end rhyme and a rhyme within the lines (an internal rhyme).

Moments fly, years move on;
Time streams by, youth has gone.

Careful thought, chosen words;
Essence caught, music heard.

Etheree

This is a ten-line poem. The first line has one syllable, the second line two syllables and so on up to ten. Or you can begin at ten syllables and work your way down to one.

Night.
Stardust
fills the sky.

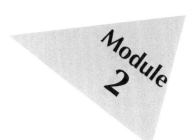

Lonely pavements,
and a few street lights,
no traffic passing by.
Lone cat peers from the hedgerow,
black as the night he inhabits.
Green moon eyes shine from his upturned face.
Heaven pours in, there just for him it seems.

Lanturne

This is a shape poem that should look like a Japanese lantern. It has five lines, and the syllables go – one, two, three, four, one.

Moon,
round gold,
fills the sky
with a soothing
light.

This
poem
strokes the page
with its soft, gentle
touch.

If you want even more of a challenge, ask your teacher for the web address of a site called Shadow Poetry.

Move on now to the next module.

Module
1

Tips for writing

(There are no teacher's notes for this module.)

Getting ready to write

Ted Hughes, one of my favourite poets, believed that children should not be taught how to write but how to say what they mean. What's your reaction to that? One thought I had was that Ted Hughes seems to believe that:

▶ every child has something to say;

▶ what you want to say is important;

▶ the whole purpose of writing is to help you get your meaning across to others.

Poetry is one way (although a very varied way) of saying what you mean. It can be a really powerful way too, because a poem is often quite short, and a lot of ideas are concentrated there. Early on in this book we talked about ways of looking at things. At the heart of all the poetry you may write there is *your particular way* of looking at things. You are unique – there has never been anybody quite like you before and there never will be again. What you mean to say is precious for that reason alone. And a poem well written makes people listen as you pour your ideas into their minds.

By the time you reach BLASTOFF! (very soon now) you will already have read and tried writing lots of different kinds of poems. The whole point of the book so far is to give you experience in playing with words and fitting them into various poetical forms. But even more than that – the activities have been trying to show you possible ways of saying what you mean. You have to become familiar with the tools before you can use them with a confident hand. So BLASTOFF! actually means aiming for the skies with everything you've learned about poetry as your vehicle.

Handy hints and helpful tips

So from now on, as you use poetry to say what you mean:

- ▶ Be very clear about what it is you want to write about.

- ▶ Have some idea of *why* you want to write about it.

- ▶ Notice how you feel. Your thoughts grow out of your feelings.

- ▶ Sit back and be aware of the movement of your thoughts in your mind.

- ▶ Let the words come together naturally. There's no need to force anything.

- ▶ Write simply, just enough to say what you mean.

- ▶ After the words come out, don't pick at them and don't judge them. Leave the work alone and go back to it later to review and revise.

That's about it. Grab your paper and pencil and BLASTOFF!

Review

Any revisions that the pupils are encouraged to make will hone their powers of discrimination and decision-making. Furthermore these developing skills will transfer from the synthesis of words in creating poetry to the analysis and appreciation of other people's work and towards an increasing perspicacity in looking at language more generally.

However, teaching pupils to be more capable handlers of language is not just a matter of competence. I still remember very clearly, after many years, the long and agonising silences during my A Level English course when our teacher, Mr Roberts, asked us what we thought of a poem he'd just read. The fact was that either we didn't know *what* we thought, or else we were too nervous to say anything for fear of 'being wrong'. On one occasion Pete Roberts read Hardy's 'The Garden Seat' and then, as we feared, asked us what we thought of it . . .

A long and increasingly tense silence followed, during which we all tried to shrink under the tables. One of our group, Dave Heap, seemed to be growing more agitated until finally, unable to hold back any longer, he announced that he thought the poem was 'crap'. There was an almost audible gasp from the rest of us and we all looked from Dave to Pete Roberts, who sat contemplatively stroking his chin. 'And why do you think that Dave?' he wondered calmly.

Dave reeled off several reasons – that the metrical pattern was trite, the tone maudlin and self-indulgent, the theme hackneyed – then sat back with arms folded defiantly. Pete thought about these comments for a few moments and then announced with a smile, 'Ladies and gentlemen, I can safely say that your A Level English course has just begun.'

Simply put, if we want pupils to say what they mean through poetry, we must encourage that same attitude when asking them to comment on other people's writing. This requires us as teachers to invite and value the pupils' opinions, then put a 'positive pressure' on them to justify what they think. It also necessitates us holding back from letting our own views dominate or jumping in to supply what we think are the right answers. And if we consider in any way that the function of poetry is to question, challenge and subvert as well as to describe, then we must be prepared for the pupils to do that and to celebrate it when it happens.

Looking back at your poem

When is your poem finished? I think that depends on many things. In one sense it may never be finished – if you mean by that that it could never be improved. Quite often when I look again at poems I wrote years ago I decide to change a word here or tweak a phrase there. That's not a bad thing because it means *I've* changed and (maybe) improved as a writer over time. On the other hand, there's no point picking at a poem just because somebody says you're supposed to 'redraft' it. If you're satisfied with the poem after you've looked back at it, leave it alone.

On the other hand . . . Wait a minute, that's three hands! OK, on the other foot, sometimes a poem comes out of my head just right, and there's nothing I feel I want to change. Even years later, that poem hits just the right note and does what I wanted it to do.

Helpful tips

So where does that leave us? See what you think about these ideas:

▶ When you write a poem, just let the words come up from your heart and out of your head. Don't try and fiddle with the poem or 'edit' it while it's being made.

▶ When it's there on the page, read it aloud a couple of times to check the sense of it and the balance of the sound. You might change a few things at this point.

▶ Leave it alone for a while. Maybe look at it again later that day or the next. Read it aloud again. How does it seem to you now? If you're pleased with it, leave it alone. If you're not, ask yourself what you might change to improve the work.

▶ Enjoy your achievement at getting this far. You've thought hard and you've been creative, and these words say something about you. Feel the pleasure at having written your poem.

▶ Listen to other people's advice, but don't automatically think that their opinions are 'better' than yours. If they suggest changes, ask them how they think that improves your work. You may find that two opinions are the opposite of one another!

- ▶ Never throw any of your work away. Keep it safe. Keep backup copies of your poems on a computer, or print them out and put them in a folder. You'll be fascinated to look back at how you felt when a poem was born.

- ▶ Learn to be a better poet by writing new poems. Even though trying to improve your old poems can teach you things, always look towards the next challenge.

The poet T. S. Eliot said that we struggle not to win or lose but to keep something alive. Perhaps you'll give some thought to that and wonder what your poetry is keeping alive?

Bibliography

Alexander, M. (1970) *The Earliest English Poems*. Harmondsworth, Middlesex: Penguin Classics Series.

Basho, M. (1985) *On Love and Barley: Haiku of Basho*. Harmondsworth, Middlesex: Penguin Classics Series.

Bowkett, S. (2007) *100+ Ideas for Teaching Creativity*. London and New York: Continuum.

Bowkett, S. (2007) *Jumpstart! Creativity*. London and New York: Routledge.

Bowkett, S. (2009) *Countdown to Creative Writing*. London and New York: Routledge.

Brownjohn, S. (1986) *Does It Have To Rhyme?* London: Hodder & Stoughton.

Brownjohn, S. (1993) *The Ability to Name Cats*. London: Hodder & Stoughton.

Causeley, C. (1974) *The Puffin Book of Magic Verse*. Harmondsworth, Middlesex: Puffin.

Corti, D. (1994) *Writing Poetry*. Nairn, Scotland: Thomas & Lochar.

Gowar, M. (1992) *Carnival of the Animals and Other Poems*. London: Viking.

Halliwell, J. O. (1970) *Popular Rhymes and Nursery Tales of England*. London: The Bodley Head.

Harding, T. (2003) *That's Science! Learning Science Through Songs*. Stafford: Network Educational Press.

Hopkins, G. M. (1970) *Poems and Prose* (ed. W. H. Gardner), Harmondsworth, Middlesex: Penguin.

Hughes, T. (1970) *Poetry in the Making*. London: Faber & Faber.

Hughes, T. (1972) *Selected Poems 1957–1967*. London: Faber & Faber.

Hughes, T. (1979) *Moortown*. London: Faber & Faber.

Moustaki, N. (2001) *The Complete Idiot's Guide to Writing Poetry*. Indianapolis, TN: Alpha Books.

Opie, I. and Opie, P. (1992) *I Saw Esau*. London: Walker Books.

Postman, N. and Weingartner, C. (1972) *Teaching as a Subversive Activity*. Harmondsworth, Middlesex: Penguin Education Specials.

Sedgwick, F. (2003) *Teaching Poetry*. London and New York: Continuum.

Stevens, W. (1993) *Selected Poems*. London: Faber & Faber.

Van Allsberg, C. (1996) *The Mysteries of Harris Burdick* (portfolio edition). Boston, MA: Houghton Mifflin.

Index

(Numbers refer to Module numbers. **Bold** numbers indicate that the topic appears in the **Teacher's notes**. Entries in *italics* refer to poems which carry *permission to be copied* for educational use. Asterisks indicate that material for this entry is available on the website.)

For Product Safety Concerns and Information please contact our EU representative GPSR@taylorandfrancis.com Taylor & Francis Verlag GmbH, Kaufingerstraße 24, 80331 München, Germany

Printed and bound by CPI Group (UK) Ltd, Croydon, CR0 4YY

11/04/2025

01843980-0007